MW00769141

horse mEdicine

A Novel by
M.C. DALLEY

revised edition

American Zen Association
New Orleans, Louisiana

Sixteen came
Sixteen died
Mice

M. C. DALLEY

PREFACE TO THE AMERICAN EDITION

The author, like the narrator, of *Horse Medicine* is a Zen monk in Paris who finds himself within two lineages: the lineage of Zen patriarchs from Bodhidharma and Dogen to the Madawaki and Yakumatsu of the novel, and the lineage of literary patriarchs from Rabelais and Celine to Henry Miller and Charles Bukowski. But M. C. Dalley is neither as celebratory as Rabelais nor as rabid as Celine; neither as bookish as Miller nor as seedy as Bukowski. He is, unspectacularly, himself.

On first reading, some readers may find, as I admit I did, the narrator of *Horse Medicine* imperfect, even unlikable: his treatment of women, his offhand racial epithets, his obsession with his own bodily and mental functions may seem self-indulgent and derivative, childish, a literary posture. But on second and third readings (and it says something that the book allows for second and third readings), these superficial blemishes give way to our fascination with the humanity underneath, the humanity of one who has found his identity in or through certain postures – the posture of zazen (or zaso, as he likes to call it) and the posture of the expatriate bohemian artist. We are all blemished, and the less we reject Mike Dalley's flaws, the more we rise not above his but *to* our own humanity. Like a monk begging during takuhatsu, Dalley bows his head to give us the opportunity to practice our understanding, perhaps even our compassion. We don't have to like him. What we have to do is to recognize in him our own posturing.

Anyone who has seriously practiced Zen will be able to appreciate the novel's descriptions of the gyoji of daily practice. The narrator claims ancestry with Rabelais and Celine, but there is no expansive historical satire here, no metaphysical jest, just one man/monk's daily experience with the corporeal realities of his own karma as he gets up every morning, makes his way somehow to the dojo, and perches on his zafu to observe the delusional nature of his passions, the stray thoughts and distractions that rise and pass during zazen, the teachings that stick and those that slide away never to be heard from again, as well as the beauty of the ceremony. It's all here: the ridiculous and the sublime – the nitty-gritty of satori.

The trouble with most "Zenmoirs," as we can call the genre of autobiographical accounts of Zen practice, is that even the best of them want to put the authors in a flattering light, as more or less insightful, self-deprecatingly witty, Zen-like (whatever that may be), or "enlightened," instead of descending into the depths of their own distastefulness, even though these depths are probably the real reason they have come to or stayed with Zen practice. From the most recent examples of Zenmoirs, all the way back to Hui-neng and Hakuin, Zen posturing is nothing new.

In American Zen this posturing often takes on a pernicious self-righteousness, a very un-bodhisattva-like tendency to turn the basis of Mahayana Buddhism, practicing for the good of the other, into a form of self-help. Dalley complains of American Zen's "bakeries and libraries and kindergartens and dojos and cafeterias and restaurants," but the real danger is in diluting the Dharma into psychodrama, right action into Puritanism, right speech into politically correct euphemism, respect for all existences into mere vegetarianism, and so on. True Buddhism, True Zen, is more vigorous than that and deserves direct action and straight talk. In the Bobo-roshi tradition of Ikkyu's "wineshop and whorehouse" poetry and Li Yu's seventeenth-century erotic novel *The Carnal Prayer Mat*, Dalley attempts to remind us that in Zen at least, if not in all forms of Buddhism, you don't have to check your genitals with your shoes at the door of the Dharma.

Unable to find a publisher willing to go against the American Buddhist grain, *Horse Medicine* was published in France in 2002 and quickly sold out its first edition. Now the American Zen Association, the only U.S. affiliate of the European-based Association Zen Internationale, has republished the novel to make it available to those who would practice the true, vigorous, unsqueamish, unflinching Zen.

A final note on the text. Regular punctuation is not one of the precepts that M. C. Dalley observes. I have made a few emendations to the French edition to correct his spelling and to clarify his cowboy punctuation, making it a little more consistent with at least itself. I have not, however, tried to "correct" his punctuation, which has its own rules. We may think of Zen monks as being more careful about such details – sweeping, sweeping – to the point of obsessive compulsion, as though Zen were a haven for the perfectionist. That's only one of many assumptions about Zen that M. C. Dalley flushes down the toilet, where all such assumptions belong.

Richard Collins
New Orleans Zen Temple
December 2002

PREFACE TO THE FRENCH EDITION

The book you are about to read might be considered strange and somewhat upsetting – at least that's what publishers seem to think, having refused it, on both sides of the Atlantic. To what genre does it belong? Spiritual or scandal sheet? Blaise Pascal or Charles Bukowski? The hero, a forty-year-old American bursting with vitality and just a bit cynical, leads a disorderly life in Paris, in which sex and alcohol figure prominently. Holed up in a seedy room, he wears himself out writing novels that every editor turns down. Nothing new here: several illustrious compatriots, including Henry Miller, have preceded him down this path. The twist lies in the fact that this bizarre individual, this "Montparnasse cowboy," is also a Zen monk, the faithful and diligent disciple of a Japanese master. Every morning, M. C. wakes up at dawn and goes to join his fellow disciples at the dojo, where, seated in meditation, each of them escapes for an instant his own madness and the madness of the world to turn into himself and listen to the master's teaching. The first-person narration of the author's tribulations is therefore punctuated by descriptions of the dojo and zazen practice, meetings with the master, thoughts about the teaching….which explains the publishers' perplexity: "How can a boozer bouncing between who-knows-how-many affairs of the heart – or of the bedroom – dare to talk about the Buddha-Way and the highest dimension of human existence? No sir, take your manuscript back and decide once and for all if you are a pornographer or a preacher."

As far as we're concerned, this rejection reflects a conformism, a lack of daring all the more regrettable since it is erroneous from both a spiritual point of view and in terms of the book's literary value. On the one hand, the quest for the Way, the aspiration to go beyond the self, brings a breath of fresh air to this tale of debaucheries and disappointments, giving it an infectious lightness and grace. On the other hand, does the distinction between the trivial and the sacred really hold up?… Taking Master Dogen at his word, Dalley makes himself the object of his own study. Obviously this approach precludes being able to shut one's eyes to reality. The author is not in the least indulgent in his rendering of the dissolute life of his hero – it is simply his lot, the path he follows in the jungle of passions and illusions that arise from within and without, the training ground where the master's teaching can blossom.

I spoke earlier about cynicism. It's true, the hero and author are perhaps a bit cynical; but only in the highest sense of the word, cynical like Diogenes, who refused to kid himself or let himself be fooled, cynical in the sense of the expression *maku mozo*, "no illusions," so dear to Zen masters. This cynicism is in no way mocking or disabused. It seeks to find the root in all things, to push aside the trappings in order to grasp what is truly at stake, which is nothing less than reality itself – *immo*, as the Zen Buddhists call it, suchness, the nature of things stripped of the fantasies and judgments that we plaster over it. And even if this search detours through deviation and excess, what of it ? Given the enormity of what's at stake, who could take offense, apart from prudes and zealots?

Yakumatsu, M. C. Dalley's Zen master, often talks about the link that unites *shiki*, phenomena, and *ku*, vacuity. Some people would like to sweep *shiki* under the rug in order to see nothing but *ku*. This is not the case for M. C. Dalley, who is an implacable observer of phenomena – not to revel in them, but to extract from them what is quintessential, justly persuaded as he is that they hold the secret to vacuity. And besides, aren't religiosity, the aspiration to purity and doctrinal certitudes themselves movements of the mind, illusions, phenomena? In this sense M. C. Dalley situates himself in the purest and highest Zen tradition. Sooner or later, we will have to admit it.

Moreover, it is from this continual rebounding from the world of phenomena to the world of the Way that the book draws its rhythm and density. It is both autobiographical novel (we could even call it a logbook, since each chapter begins with waking up and ends with going to sleep) and spiritual adventure, the story of a quest for wisdom, authenticity, freedom and harmony, where, in the most unexpected moments, a completely original and disconcerting teaching shows through, a lucid teaching that cuts to the root of our illusions and deepest aspirations. It is in the mouth of madness, in the eye of the cyclone, that M. C. suddenly finds the intimate calm and certitude of the perfection of all things. Certainly, the author is walking a tightrope, bringing us to the edge of the abyss. But just when the narrative seems on the verge of becoming trivial or unbearable, silence takes over, and the clouds disperse to leave room for calm and joy.

But it is not only the themes that are innovative; it is the writing as well. Dalley invented his style and punctuation. A far cry from being formal, this punctuation follows the rhythm of thought and action – of breathing, one could say. When the story becomes panicked, when the narrator's thoughts are so swept up in torment that he no longer has time to breathe, the punctuation disappears, only to reappear further on, discreet and natural. This same natural quality quietly finds its way into the style – bare, unaffected, steering clear of preciosity as well as lyricism – so that it comes to resemble spoken language, or the private language we keep to ourselves. But make no mistake: a great mastery of the writer's craft is necessary to arrive at such simplicity. Those who doubt need only note the poetic quality that emanates from certain descriptions of Paris in the early hours, or the avowal of certain emotions.

Days go by and do not resemble each other. Each morning, each sex scene, each meditation brings something new. And the organization is brilliant: days and experiences fit together seamlessly, thanks to the introduction of objects or landmarks, of words that return like a refrain, of small events that recur unexpectedly and leave the impression of familiarity. Our interest never wanes, so well-constructed are the dialogues, so disconcerting the interactions with the master, and so fascinating the characters who appear from one chapter to another.

The impression of familiarity I just mentioned is again reinforced by the way in which the author depicts himself, without smugness, but with ravaging humor, running around "like a rabbit in heat." This character – unhappy, failed, at loose ends, sexually obsessed, drunk, aggressive, possessing nothing that he hasn't stolen or which hasn't been given to him, always looking for a 10-franc note to buy himself a beer, enjoying the company of dropouts and misfits – does not bother us. We are never tempted to measure ourselves against him: How could we feel threatened by one so lost? And yet, without knowing it, and by his very humility, he becomes our brother, our mirror on the world, and the progress that he makes on the Way that he practices becomes ours as well.

In a word, the time when spirituality constituted a separate genre, relegated to edifying works, is long gone. M. C. Dalley proves that spirituality now has its place in romanesque literature, that it mixes well with real-life experience and that it is not afraid of scandal. *Horse Medicine* reconciles with remarkable ease the spiritual and the literary, madness and wisdom, the profane and the sacred. And if you still don't know what shelf to put it on, follow my advice and open a new section on your bookshelf, because the kind of writing it embodies is, in my opinion, destined to supply a completely separate literary genre. Not to mention M. C. Dalley, who has not said his last word, and who has other works in reserve.

Luc Boussard
September 2000

PROLOGUE

Zen Buddhism is not something you talk about, write about or even read about. It is something you do, you act out, you perform. Something you live, with body and mind undivided. It is not a relative affair, but an absolute one. That is to say, something which has no opposite, no contradiction. Therefore, it would seem that there is no right or wrong, good or bad, moral or immoral, holy or profane in this life, this existence. It has nothing of the opposite in it. Cling to love and you have hate, cling to the good and you have the bad, cling to God and you have the Devil. Life is one, God and Devil together. If things are not so, and you have God on one side and the Devil on the other, you simply create division. You create the good and the bad. In religion you take up the side of piety, and what happens? Immediately you have the other side, that of profanity. You define what you are by what you are not. So the person who lives the holy life lives it in relation to the unholy life.

By bringing in the opposite of anything, you falsify everything, even existence itself. By falsifying existence, you create not only conflict, torture and war, but death itself, the death of existence. And seeing that two relative things are equal to one another in weight, strength, substance and even essence – as are all relative things – black and white, Arab and Jew, country and country – it's like fighting with your own shadow, forever. Now what can be worse than that, I wonder ?

During the Tang dynasty when the practice of zen was at its best, Tanka, a travelling monk and disciple of both Baso and Sekito, stopped off one night at a Buddhist temple in Peking. It was mid-winter and it was cold as the devil and Tanka spotted three wooden buddha statues in the buddha hall, and seizing up the biggest of the three, he made a Himalayan fire with it. He hoisted up his robe and was in the process of warming his bare ass over the flames, when suddenly the Abbot entered the hall.

"For the love of Buddha!" cried the Abbot. "You have burned him!"

Tanka dropped his robe, turned around and began poking about in the ashes, as if searching for something.

"What are you up to now, monk?" shouted the Abbot.

"I'm looking for the sarira (i.e., the remains or bits of bone-matter of a cremated Buddha). I wish to collect them."

"You must be completely crazy! A wooden statue doesn't have sarira!"

"In that case," replied the monk, "why don't we burn the other statues as well. You know, Abbot, it's very cold tonight and the Buddha within is shivering."

"No, no, I am sorry but you must leave. Now get out! And to the devil with you!" This said, the Abbot opened the door and Tanka left. Walked off into the freezing night.

François Rabelais lived the same dilemma. In his premonitory "Prologue to the Reader," he writes how the publication of *Pantagruel* leaves him wavering between hope and fear, uncertain whether he may not meet with an unpleasant reception instead of the appreciation he expects. "Instead of doing the readers a service," he writes,

18

"I may offend them; instead of amusing them, annoy them; instead of pleasing them, displease them. Mine may be the fate of Euclid's cock… the creature that discovered the treasure with his scratching and had his throat cut for his pains. Would it not be distressing if that were to happen to me? Such a thing has happened before; it could easily happen again…"

1

> There I am, frozen stiff, nothing to get me
> warm except a couple hours' long-distance
> running before breakfast, not even a slice of
> bread-and-sheepdip.
>
> A. SILLITOE, *The Loneliness of the Long-
> Distance Runner*

I am dreaming, my wife is cutting my hair. Hurry
hurry you're taking too long, I am going to miss the bell
the doors will be locked. The thought wakes me with a
start, I jump up, turn on the light, holy shit the alarm did-
n't ring. Twelve-to-seven I have four minutes and thirty
seconds to get out of here.

What's happening? – a voice from the bed. / Go back
to sleep sweetheart, I've gotta move. / Huh? What? What
time is it?

The lady rubs her eyes and yawns and stretches and I
think to myself, just my luck, another slow one. What time
is it? she asks, squinting at the clock with the lousy ring.
Ah me too! she declares and jumps out of bed and now we
are both standing freezing in the room... No time for coffee, I say jerking back the curtain, No time to put on the
heat. Brrr it's bloody freezing in here, but there's no time
no time, not even for trembling coughing or sneezing, no
time for anything in this world, by God. You have any coffee in this place? asks the lady. I ignore her and pull on my
shorts – found them six years ago at my wife's, man's
shorts to be sure, – my wife's lover's underpants but not

mine – never mind – I mean, imagine forgetting your underpants somewhere, man, some people just don't care about anything. Then into my pants grey flannels a gift from Bernie the pants salesman, and my undershirt and black turtleneck both gifts from my friend Lee, and the socks a gift from my friend and literary coach Chevalier, and the boots a gift from my old girlfriend Anne who got them from her former lover who bought them on sale in Barbès – but that was a long time ago and the boots are in sad shape nowadays the right one is held together with glue so I slip it on slowly despite my present state of anguish and doubt. Then I rush into the kitchen piss in the sink wash my face and drink some hot water. (Yaku says, drink hot water in the morning, it keeps you from coughing)… Man I hope the lady Whatshername doesn't blow it, women can be so darn slow… I stick my hand out the kitchen window nope no rain this morning, that's something new! Crash back into the room leaving the window open behind me snatch up my rakusu, a gift from Yaku, my master and my man, loop it over my head with one hand, pull my jacket off the nail in the door with the other – a black leather jacket a gift from Margot; nice jacket but it is falling apart and my arm gets tangled up in the sleeve and I rip my way right through no time to waste on jacket linings right now and open the door – Hey! Are you ready or what?

Oui oui! says the lady perkily stepping through the door. Well how do you like that she is ready alright, ready to kill in her brown boots, tight corduroys and fur coat open at the waist. Must be the racing-car driver in her, that's what she used to do she told me so last night, a real speedy chick, first she raced cars, then she became an ambulance driver, and that's how she met her husband Doctor Dupont or something, can't recall his exact name but it doesn't matter they have since been divorced, and all this activity before her 25th birthday which was yesterday or tomorrow, can't recall the date but never mind. We are hopping down the stairs two at a time and she is ahead of me. And how did she do that? By not washing her face, by not brushing her teeth or not even pissing! Whatwith all those beers we drank at the Sélect last night, got to hand it to her.

I look at my watch – the watch is really my daughter's and it is on loan – but it's got one of those little girlie watch-faces and it's still pitch dark down here in the street and hard to read. Four minutes since we awoke four minutes ago in the solitary unknown and now exploding into life under a dark sky saying our goodbyes, kiss-kiss and where are you heading? me I am going this way, you are going that way, out there outside of Paris, in the banlieu some-where – the lady has her child waiting out there and soon it will be time for kindergarten and off we go into the dark, she outside the city and myself down the inside along Ray-mond-Losserand past the garbage collectors yanking and banging the tin cans past some poor bugger sleeping in a cardboard box, all the closed shutters of the shops, the Marchand de couleur, the Boulangerie, feeling pretty much alone again.

I break into a run, like dozens of others are doing right this minute, all to converge in the same place at the same time in the land where everything is better…

There are two dojos in the courtyard, one for the sitting the other for the soup. The soup dojo is also used as a cloak-room and this is where I am right now, poking around in the closet looking for my kolomo and André Dupuis the co-pilot for Air France and X the ex-terrorist and Pascal Fardet the editor shove by and out the door ahead of me. I have now located my kolomo, slip it on, grab my rakusu and run barefoot over the cold cement across the frozen grass around the boney tree under a tiny windbell hanging in the doorway, across the gaitan, the entrance area, full with people in all the nooks-and-crannies, in through the thick yellowish curtain, bow quickly to the Buddha and to all the heavenly beings and the hell people everywhere, on the ground floor, in the overhead gallery, on the stairs, and grab the last available seat between the pillar on my right and Shubert the street guitarist on my left. I plop down my zafu and sit. Bong! goes the gong, and click! goes the lock on the door, 7:30 on the dot. Anyway, the gong is still resounding and now it mingles with the sound of the inkin, the little bell tinkling tinkling faintly and purely in the yard beyond. We are ready, says the gong; okay, replies the inkin, the master is coming.

So the inkin-ringer leads the master and his secretary into the dojo. Can't see them our backs are turned but it happens every morning and we all know the ritual, like an ancient tradition impregnated in the modern time.

Those who sit on the gaitan, grumbles the master, are only mini-people... (The thing is, one is generally not allowed to sit in the entrance, but some do so anyway because it is behind the curtain and they can sit and pick their noses and fart their hearts out well away from the eye of the master and the blows of the stickman.)

Thirty or so minutes later, no one having budged a millimeter, Yakumatsu the master begins the teaching. He has been talking as of late of *Raihai Tokuzui* which means doing prostrations and attaining the marrow, and he says: You should not be concerned with the difference between the sexes. If a girl of seven has attained the Way then even an old man who has been a monk for one hundred years must do prostration to her…

Sure, it makes no difference if a master be a woman, man or even a beast, a master is a master. Be this as it may, back in thirteenth-century Japan there were no female masters, let alone female disciples – in fact women were not even allowed into the monasteries in those days. Same with master Dogen, he wasn't allowed anywhere. The thing is, the teaching he had brought back with him from China was very revolutionary: it had nothing to do with *anything* and this was just too much to take. Who was he kidding? In fact Dogen's boat had just docked in Edo and he was met on the quay by a group of officials, the Emperor's emissary and a couple of Yes-Sir abbots and, well, the emissary stepped forward and asked: Monk Dogen, what have you brought back with you? / There is nothing, replied monk Dogen, I have come back empty-handed.

The word spread real fast – Dogen's got nothing. And by the time he arrived in Kyoto all the doors, even those of the temples and monasteries where he had once practiced, were closed to him. No one would listen to him – who wants to listen to nothing! – No one would put him up, not even for the night, so he got this idea and he knocked on the door of an all-woman monastery and right-off they took him in, and they bedded him, fed him and even practiced with him. So this is why later in life he wrote the *Raihai Tokuzui* in praise of what he called the pretty sisters.

The bell is struck and everyone jumps to their feet shoving and pushing like people are prone to do and push their way up front for the ceremony. The thing is, it's important to be up in the front because then the master can see you. Anyway, I am up and on my feet and heading forward, like everyone else, but with a bit more delicacy of course, I mean I don't block, elbow or step on anyone's feet and, well, damn if I don't find myself up front with the others today. Right by the Buddha altar and feeling good about it too. I glance at the Buddha statue (a plastic imitation – the fancy bronze Buddha was stolen a few weeks ago but that's another story) and look over the Buddha's bun on top of its head and look at all the pretty sisters lined up opposite, just like in a... Why here SHE is, just the sight of her and there's this tightening in the belly...

We chant the *Hannya Shingyo* hypno-staccato and go down in prostration, and the master says Good morning! and heads out the door behind the inkin-ringer on his way to the other dojo for the genmai soup, and the shoving starts all over again... Squatting Jap style at the long low tables 40 or 50 of us in front of our bowls, we chant the *Bussho Kapila* the longest sutra of the lot; then we hold the bowls in our hands and scoop up the mushy rice and swallow it down without a word. Once the soup is finished, the silence is interrupted with a sudden burst of chatter and jokes. A dozen or so head for the door, another dozen light up cigarettes and gather on the floor around the master's table. We talk about the kusen (the teaching) and about other things, but today I keep my mouth shut, which is just as well, Yakumatsu is angry with me as of late – he doesn't like his disciples to carry on love affairs with each other and then too there's this thing about my not working – not writing – for him anymore, about my quitting on him, too much work I tell you, I mean a fellow's got to take a break now-and-then isn't that so, like a vacation or something, ah what the hell, I head for the door – the back door – to avoid paying the four-franc soup-charge – another good reason to be angry with me, but what the hell, four francs is four francs, and I slip out like greased lightning into the greasy Parisian morning, dumb grey and miserable.

Off I go to the usual place the café on the corner, shove my way through the crowd of people – I'm getting pretty good at shoving – and the patron says Good morning Monsieur Dallé a coffee or a glass of water today?

I have four extra francs on me so I say One coffee please and make it *black*. I give the patron his four francs, the four I should have given Yakumatsu… ah so what? I mean what's done is done. Besides rice mush may be healthy for you but coffee tastes better.

Then I remember, and look up. Where is she? Ah wouldn't you know it, she is standing right next to me. Now if that isn't proof she still loves me. Her back is turned and I admire it, its airy grace and all that. Bonjour I say. No reply. Doesn't even turn around. So now I think she doesn't love me, she hates me. Bonjour I say again. Nothing. Just the back of her head. I look at the back of her head for a long time.

Wanna drink?... It's old Lee from Texas, a handsome, tall, greyhaired gentleman with cowboy hat and a convertible white Daimler outside, and we drink our beer – one Tuborg and one ordinaire – and he asks me how it's going with my new girlfriend (he means the ex-racing driver) and I reply, She's not my girlfriend, I don't even know her name. Well, whoever she is, says he sipping his Tuborg, she looks alright to me…

She is gone and Lee is gone and so is everyone else and alone again I order a beer, light a cigarette, cough, give the patron his six francs, drink down the beer, leave a fifty-centime tip and head out, okay this is it, won't spend another centime there's spaghetti at the house and one full bottle of okay wine. I pass by the empty garbage cans, pass the now empty cardboard box, pass the supermarket, ah hell one bottle isn't enough. I enter the neoned hole pick up a cheap wine for six francs thirty and hit the pavement adding, four plus seven plus six is seventeen, why the day has hardly begun and I am already spent out.

2

The merit and worth of zen really lies in
whorehouses and wineshops.

IKKYU

The alarm goes off ten minutes early and the first
thing I feel is my cock so hard it hurts, wonder what
caused that, no dreams this morning no fucking last
night ah maybe that's it, couldn't get it up last night
nohow, delayed reaction, all those cigarettes and all that
wine. Well, that's how it goes, sleep is over and the
world is not quite here yet and I enter it cock at the
helm… I look down at the lady sleeping on her stomach,
doesn't plan to get up with any crazy leaps this morning
once was enough for her. Sure, that's car racing for you
– it is a one-shot affair, not like the Dharma at all.

Well, I roll the lady over, spread her thighs and try
to stick it in. But the hole is dry so I get up and rub some
margarine on the top of my cock. Then I wedge her legs
apart with my knees bent and in the Japanese kneeling
position I sink myself deep into the sleepy hothouse. The
lady moans softly but nothing more she never really
wakes up at all, which is just as well cause now I can give
it to her the way I like, without preamble frivolities or
postscript, just a "Dear lady, love Mike" kind of missile
I mean missal, just three long strokes and unload.

I light a match and turn on the heat a butagaz contraption which blows out a lot of stinking gas and a little
line of heat. Then wash off my cock and examine my face

29

in the mirror. Needs a shave, and the hair a brushing. I go through dokan, the routine, shake some dry shampoo on my head rub it in, douse some eau de cologne under my arms on my neck and shaved cheeks – it's important not to stink up the dojo, like Spinacio and other clods we know.

What is that? A mouse! Goddam, he's the culprit who has been eating my spaghetti... Time for coffee but there is no coffee, only wine. I pour myself a glass, sit down on a zafu in the middle of the floor, roll myself a cigarette and stare out the windowpane. What a pathetic sight. I mean there is good reason to be depressed sometimes, like right now, I mean the sky, the light (if that is what you call it), is straight dishwater.

Not too cold in the street for a change. It's been a hard winter, but today is February the fourth and we will be able to warm our tootsies in a sort of sun soon... Not quite awake yet... must be the wine... I enter a café and order a double coffee. Now wasn't that a good thing the alarm went off early? time to dally, time to think. Think of what? of HER biensûr. God have mercy on this poor sod he has done all a man can do to control and solidify this mind and what has he discovered? She is inside it and there is abolutely no way to shake her out. Sit every day in zazen, as I have done, and look where it gets you. I mean ten years with Yaku and I have not even made first base haven't even hit the ball yet, still swinging wide. Well maybe it is not really all my fault. Maybe Yaku is not such a hot teacher after all, I mean haven't I followed Yaku correctly am I not one of his disciples too?... Or is it I have not followed him correctly after all? Not writing for him anymore, not paying for the soup… Yes, this is more likely, yes I can see it now how great is the Dharma and how insignificant is me the man…

Approaching the dojo my mind changes and now, as always, it is thinking of the teaching, Yaku has finished his morning commentaries of *Raihai* and now the brain is wondering what is on the agenda for today. I make the last fifty-meter stretch running.

I enter the dojo going fast, conscious as usual of my body which is comfortable and agile, in through the left side of the door – never enter through the middle or on the right – zafu tucked under my arm, like a football, bow sharply to the Buddha and the others, Howdy-do mates! step in front of some dojo hang-asses dragging feet, spot a seat by the post, and still in the ballgame I smack down the old zafu for a touchdown. Bow again, sit on the ball and look at my watch…

Seated up front is my sometimes friend Ambrosio an editor at Albin Michel. He once tried to get me edited, showed my manuscript to Nabokov's son or something, a failed writer-become-editor like the rest of them, the failed writers I mean, and Nabokov could tell just by flipping through the pages that the book stank, And, well, one day we were over at the temple – it was after a sesshin and we must have been drunk or something – and we got to talking and I hit Ambrosio in the neck, don't know why, it must have been the alcohol, a couple of drinks and every precept in the Buddhist Canon goes down the drain… And here is Tamponard sitting to my left. Farmboy hick though you would never know it going by his credentials – he's a product of l'Ecole Normale Superieure in math. I don't know Tamponard very well he keeps clear of me for some reason, maybe I intimidate him, who knows... But I do remember the time Tamponard went on a drunk, lasted six months night and day and near the end the mathematician was on all fours outside the dojo vomiting and cussing out everybody on their way in and out. And here comes Smartie the gadfly, pops up just before the bell and takes the empty place behind me – another editor of sorts, works with three or four publishers at a time, puts out books with his own name on them, on Buddhism Hinduism Yoga Astrology Clairvoyance you name it... Well it is a very distinguished and elite crowd round-about me this morning flesh-and-blood editors, drunken mathematicians, and a mystico gadfly.

Zazen begins, lots of wind and lightning, must be from that double coffee, can wind you up like a speed-freak. Now that is what happens when you have time on your hands, when the alarm goes off too early, more time to think shit, more time to mumble into your coffee cup... Okay close the eyes. No they won't close. Can't even close my own eyes today they pop right open again. Okay try the breathing breathe deeply. Can't do that either it is all stuck in the thorax...

The wind has died away and the lightning has let up; the weather has changed – Don't know when though, don't know how long we have been sitting here, never even noticed. Mind changes and there is no one around to notice the change. Time-and-space sure is a strange thing even if my death comes to me right now it won't matter really, I am already in the coffin.

Lamponéon! Do gassho when you cough! says the master to his closest disciple, and everyone jumps; the master has gone and disturbed everybody in their nice little samadhis and for what? The coughing didn't bother me... Gassho is very important, the master goes on about gassho, but if you do not want to do gassho in front of the Buddha statue or to me or to the others here, then please do it to yourself in front of your mirror.

Gassho is a gesture with hands joined palm to palm in front of the breast... and I see what he means. It is a way to cut through the ego, and anyway it's the gesture itself which counts not the object of the gesture, it is the brain which counts and the gesture of the hands goes right there, to the brain.

This dojo is empty today, says Sensei. On the gallery there is only one person. People are tired on Thursdays and they do not come. Many of my disciples who hold important positions in this dojo come only once a week. They arrive only on the day they are scheduled to do the kyosaku. These people, he roars, ARE NO LONGER TO DO THE KYOSAKU!

Now that's right, I think to myself, those sag-asses should all be sacked... Funny how everyone is the same the world over, even in holy places. Give a man a little title and...

ALL MONKS WHO HAVE LITTLE OF DENDOSHI, he roars again, AND WHO NO LONGER WORK TO SPREAD ZAZEN WILL LOSE THEIR TITLES!

Right on! I think to myself… Well, maybe I think this way because I am not a dendoshi myself. To be a dendoshi you must be registered as such at Eiheiji in Japan, and to tell the truth I don't give a hoot about being a dendoshi. Don't give a hoot about spreading zazen either. Not much for proselytizing myself. Let the people be, let them fart their lives away, be my guest, do as you please, I am no bodhisattva, have no wish to save the world, the world can go to hell, I mean why should I worry? I have my master, my dojo and my sangha, and the sangha, the community, is big enough as it is, one more man in this place and we will die like sardines. I mean, who wants more? We have enough as it is… As it is, what with all these people around the master, people like myself… but, maybe the master is thinking he could do better with another bunch; sure, that's why he wants us to work to spread zazen, maybe this way old Yaku will catch the big fish he can't with us, not in a sardine can anyhow.

The quality of disciples, the mind of masters – who cares? My belly is smooth and tight and round as a tadpole's my shoulders are down like they should be, like a broken axle, my back is erect and so is my neck like a swan's neck, it's the last act, the swan song, that's how it is, every zazen is the last and final one, this is why nothing matters…

The kyosaku hits someone's shoulder, ka-thump ka-thump! Then the other kyosaku, plifff, plifff. Must be a girl wielding that one… ah no, it's André Dupuis the airline pilot… the pilot has no hara no ki at all. Probably got top grades though, sat up front in class, polished the apple and… well that's modern education for you, nothing to do with hara, ki or cock and balls, and you can fly skyhigh nowadays.

Someone is pushing down on my left shoulder, hunh it's Yakumatsu I know the touch. So my posture is not so good today? My left shoulder too high? Hunh and all along I thought I was sitting perfect as a buddha. Well that's what happens, the posture shows you inside-out, and if you are like me and not in the best of heads, it will show, like right now, right now my head is in my left shoulder, making me lopsided…

The master is talking. He is reading a letter from Bistourix, one of his disciples down in Africa. This disciple has written several books on zen and now he has written to the master to tell him that he, Yaku, is not a true master, but a false one a fake… People like Bistourix who write books on zen are foolish, foolish, says Yaku: Every day in the minds of human beings comes the wind which brings the waves. People who write stories are inspired by these waves and this is unhealthy it is muso, muso of their own consciousness, it is the mind which floats and always is agitated by the environment.

Well that's me he's talking about this time. Stir up all the phenomena, seek after it, capture it, subjugate, tame, mold, breed and sell it… What was so great about a Fitzgerald, Steinbeck or Faulkner besides what they sold? Also, Plato sold Socrates, Buddhagosha sold Buddha…, why the man who writes, it would seem, stands on the shoulders of those who don't…

The bell for kinhin is struck and we are walking slowly in a line like black shadows of death and wouldn't you know it – here SHE is, right smack in front of me and my eyes are on her thighs and there is nothing I can do about it, my cock twitches in my frock and I have this picture of myself throwing up her robe and kesa and taking her doggie-style, right now during kinhin, by God I slam it in her like nobody's business, serves her right the bitch, I mean it's like the master says, writers are agitated by the environment, I mean what's the difference between a holy place and a whorehouse, it's all in the head anyway – agitated, agitating...

The master has just said something funny and people are laughing, squirming on their butts and blowing their noses, people in this burlesco will laugh at anything. "Now beginning tomorrow," says Yakumatsu once the laughing dies down, "I will begin *Shinjin Gakudo*, which means body and mind, studying the Way..."

All of us pile out the door behind the master happy zazen is over with – that's the nicest thing about doing zazen once you get it over with you feel pretty good – and Gaitan the wise-ass pushes Yvonne of the big tits into a puddle and the master hits Wise-ass hard on the head with his kotsu and someone else does this and someone else does that, and who cares, just a bunch of disciples acting rowdy and wild (reminds me of Ennin, the Japanese Marco Polo of the 800s who visited the Chan monastery of Hyakujo, then wrote a chronicle concerning twenty-one Chan monks he met on several occasions, summing them up as 'extremely unruly men at heart'), and we enter the sliding doors into the room of steaming brown rice boiled with carrots and other things, a sticky goo, the bowls are filled to the brim with it and Gaitan gobbles his up and asks for seconds. Me, I don't much like the stuff, eat half a bowl and the sweat breaks out on my forehead, a tremor runs through my body and I feel the vomit coming. I clench my fists and clench my teeth and screw my eyes closed and when I open them again, the tremor having passed I see *her*, across the table, eating her soup with such grace, with a slight beckoning smile, like a sexy Botticelli and right off I want her again. I can feel it right to the bottom of my balls. Disgusted with myself (is there no more to me but a mouth for to eat, an asshole for to shit and a cock for to copulate?) I quickly pay my four francs, remove my robe jerk on my jeans walk straight out and straight over to the Marchand de couleur on Losserand where I buy myself a mousetrap. Then I drop by the post office, pick up a package of books I left behind at Maddux's place in North Carolina last month, and head for the café.

A little late for the café, it's ten-ten and most everyone has gone off to work. Apart from Tamponard and Buchembois both still drunk from the night before and unwinding on beer, one in his eternal red-plaid lumberjacket, the other in his baggy cotton pants not made for these winter temperatures, and a very pale man dressed in what looks like a burlap bag, and the waiter in black and white, and the patron, the boss, also in his clothes, apart from that there is no one. The boss asks me if I want a coffee today, No more today, merci, says I, the package of books under my arm, the mousetrap on the counter before me. I've spent enough today I'll just take a glass of hot water if you don't mind – drink hot water in the morning, it's good for you – and while I am sipping my hot water the boss looks at my mousetrap. You know how to bait this thing? First you've got to remove the human odors, how do you remove the human odors? with chloride. And to set the trap you must wear rubber gloves. Rubber gloves?... I thank the boss for the information and thank him too for the water, and on my way home, passing all kinds of nice pretty ripe things, turning my head to look after their hot young bodies, I remember Mrs. Whatshername! I had forgotten her. A wave of desire surges over me. I look at my watch, wonder if she's still there, wonder if she's waiting for me, waiting in bed, you know with her legs wide apart and all, oh I hope so, I hope so! I enter the Boulangerie, bonjour monsieur! bonjour mam'oiselle! and purchase two croissants one for me and one for her and somehow I can read the writing in the face of the Boulangère – Mrs. Whatshername is waiting for me! – and at the same time I count out the money four francs and something, merci monsieur merci mam'oiselle, yes that makes a total of ten francs thirty man if we're not more careful we will never get that new pair of shorts.

I walk up the stairs, pulling up my shirt collar, combing my hair with my fingers and I enter the room and of course she is still here, just as I had hoped, a well-rested housewife in the big bad bed, and we look at one another and there is no mistaking it, her legs are spread under the covers knees raised and I drop the pack of books and the mousetrap and the croissants and say: Oh I'm sure glad you're here. /Moi aussi, Michael, I've been thinking about you. And you? / Biensûr, I reply sitting down on the bed. We exchange a few words, not much, Caroline – that's her name, Caroline – isn't much of a talker, I mean she never asks me anything, don't really believe she thinks about me when I'm not about, probably not, she's just gone through a divorce with a real bastard and anyway what woman in her right mind would ever want to hook up with me, I dunno. At least not on a steady diet.

My cock is big and hard as a kotsu, it's that zazen energy, goes right to the cock that's the truth…, and well I pull back the covers, ever so gently – I'm not that crude, I mean I don't rip them off and ram it up to the balls, like in a porno show – and I slip ever so close and give her my body heat – or rather I take hers, I mean I got hara and ki and a fast metabolism but for some reason my body is always on the cold side, maybe it's I don't eat enough – and I carefully caress her thighs, outside and in.

Now I will tell you what I do next (and mind you I apologize in advance – no, not only in advance, but after the very fact as well; I mean if a man is to apologize for the mere *writing* of it, then he must apologize, and even more so, for having done it in the first place!) so this said I stick one finger into her cunt, and while we talk, I stick the other up her asshole. Meanwhile, somehow managing to maintain a semblance of proper decor and civility, we talk about us, about how good we are for one another, especially now etc. etc., and she agrees, says she wants it to go on this way, and I go on, go on playing with her cunt and asshole, taking it easy, looking her over. Not much in the way of tits but she has thighs and buttocks that can handle plenty and, to make a long take short, I get myself into the correct posture for the insertion and she helps it along by spreading apart her cuntlips and in we go in up to the balls and yowie! we go hard at it beating banging and dancing to the music don't know how long…

3

What good is doing zazen? Good for nothing!
Unless you make callouses in your ears and
genuinely do the good-for-nothing you never
become anything.

MADAWAKI

Seven-oh-seven, having coffee and listening vaguely to
the music coming over the new radio, a present from Caroline, a fine woman really, maybe we will get to know one
another one of these days, I mean it's a great radio with lots
of buttons and dials and fun to play with too, catch a song
here-and-there, a Paul McCartney with his usual senti-
mental slop, a little bit on the atomic bomb over Hiroshima
– did you know that the light of the explosion is said to
have appeared brighter than a thousand suns? Sure, and
what did it light up exactly? In light there is obscurity, said
master Tozan… And the weather report, in obscurity there
is light… What I mean is, there's nothing wrong with
radios, it's what you do with them that counts. After all the
Buddha Shakyamuni was a little like a radio himself, a
kind of transmitter. Gave a good broadcast. You can still
hear it today.

I glance at my daughter's watch, got to hit the road. On
the way to the door I take a quick look at myself in the big
broken mirror, check out the few-days growth on my face,
eyes all bloodshot from last night's bout at the bar, last
night with HER at the Café du Château, God that was awful,
the little bitch, but there's no time for thinking about that

now, and anyway who cares, I do gassho to this reflection which is not me, that just can't be me, and split.

The sky is a horrible daybreak-grey, spattered here and there with clouds reminiscent of smoke-globs from a rubber factory, but that too is Buddha thinks I, hopping over a puddle in the sidewalk, twelve-past-seven and there's more light in the sky at this time than there was yesterday at this same second. Spring is coming.

I'm in the dressing room yanking on my black robe, (it's not exactly 'my' black robe, it's Ramon's, the macrobiotic journalist who doesn't come here anymore because his wife said it's either me or the master, make your choice, be a true husband or a true monk, and Ramon actually made the choice, he took her). So I am dressing in Ramon's robe and not talking to anyone, don't care to talk in the mornings, before zazen, but Tamponard who is pulling on his own rather motley grey-black robe says: Hey Mike, was that you making all that racket last night? / What? / A drunk American was in the streets swearing and cussing and throwing things. / Nope it wasn't me. / Tiens! He had your exact Yankee accent I'd swear to it, you sure it wasn't you? / No man it wasn't me.

I take a seat on the other side of the dojo, near the master and the girls, and glance at my watch. Earlier than usual, there are still a few minutes to go and the spaces about me are not yet filled. Some people even play it closer to the line than myself… I think of the night before, don't recall throwing things, no, I went straight home, didn't even have dinner, not even Caroline's leftover croissant, too fucked up, couldn't eat, just fell dressed in the bed, like into a crater, fell out for three hours, woke up for no reason at all, must have been my unconscious messing up again, flicked on the light and read up on the *Shinjin Gakudo*, the teaching to begin today... Ah there's Vanessa and Martinette. Both smile and sit down. Another woman also in a black kimono sits down in front of me, a professional dancer they say, can't recall her name, great legs though, not toothpicks. The space to my left is filled by whatzename Doctor Kraut, perfumed immaculate trimmed beard straight-jacketed into his well-tailored robe. Ah here is Mama Yvonne big-assed and titty, a kimono with something in it. And Smartie editor of things spiritual, just published another book on Buddhism – one thing you can say about Smartie, he's smart enough to make his practice pay – and he walks right up to the translator's spot and sits down. What is he doing in the translator's seat? that's not his job! Anyway Smartie takes up the posture and avoiding the eyes of those sitting four rows thick in front, he arranges his kolomo about his knees like everything is alright which of course it isn't since Smartie is going to get the boot any minute now and he knows it too, he must know it, he's been round here as long as me. Sure people think he is vain or something but I think he is just crazy, I mean you have to be crazy to play vain when it's clear that very soon you are going to be told to beat it, and you are going to beat it, in front of everyone, because the show can't go on otherwise. Well I kind of feel sorry for the guy, I know what he is going through, mix with spiritual stuff too much and you go bananas just like that. I mean I know another guy who practiced zen Buddhism,

43

Lamaism, Vipassana and yoga and today he is in the loonybin,... Anyway the kyosakuman picks the stick off the altar saunters over and pokes the old poke in the back with it and says: Dégage, scram, beat it. Oh the humiliation I can't look at his face.

Only after the bell is struck and directly before the door is locked does Lucien Dagoba the real translator arrive and take up the already heated seat. Today we are in good hands Alphonse Lamponéon is on the kyosaku and Dagoba is giving the French rendition of the master's words, two of the best.

The little bell goes tinkle tinkle and the master and his secretary arrive with a swish of kolomos. After a long silence lasting through the entire first part, through kinhin and into the middle of the second sitting that is about 45 or 50 minutes, he says: "Certainly it is difficult to come here to zazen every morning especially when you live in the social world; those who continue to practice zazen here every morning – you are true great men great women, you will have a big influence on society and the world."

Yakumatsu begins the oral teaching by promulgating the *Shinjin Gakudo*, study done through the mind and study done through the body and the necessity of harmonizing practice with satori, and how satori is not satori, there is no satori for to promulgate the Dharma one must forget the self…, sure forget forget I have forgotten everything even what comes next, too dense a dose for my brain right now, Jesus if there is anything god damn intellectual in this world it is that god damn Dogen.

The ceremony, SHE is not here this morning and my eyes wander freely over the faces; we are standing, the master is saying something, and we go down in sanpai, the three prostrations, dropping our knees and hitting our forehead on the hard floor, and right this moment I am feeling euphoric, guess it has something to do with the sanpai posture itself, doing what all the wise and the holy do, like Baso who banged his head so hard on the ground for so many years that he had a forehead big and hard as a coconut, and I lift my eyes before the others and look at them all with their heads down on the ground and what do I see? I see a golden light emanating about them, no kidding, it's enough to bring tears to your eyes...

Genmai is over, Yaku gestures for me to sit down beside him, and I squat down on my knees, and without further ado he hands me a few pages full of handwriting and says, You must help me, yes?

I have been avoiding Yaku lately, I don't want to help him anymore, I want to help myself, but I feel bad, I have this rotten selfish attitude and what the heck, I nod and say sure, sure, take the pencil offered me by Virginie and go over the words. It's the teaching he gave this morning. I am trying hard to concentrate but there is so much going on, Yaku is talking with Virginie his secretary and everyone else is talking too, and a Japanese man who turns out to be an emissary from the Japanese Embassy shows up and Sensei greets the man in Japanese and the latter kneels down discreetly at the other table and the master is now talking to Viviane, Smartie's wife, and he has completely forgotten about the Japanese emissary, and others come up, all disciples, with this-and-that on their minds, and one of them says he is in love with two girls at the same time and what should he do, if he doesn't leave one he will lose the other while if he does leave one he will still lose the other, and everybody breaks out laughing even Yaku, it's too much, and someone else cuts off the troubled lover to ask about headaches: Does zazen cure headaches Sensei? Sensei doesn't bother to even answer this nitwit but someone else does, someone else says "Hell Zazen *gives me* headaches," and I look up from my work and say "Yes hearing Dogen is harder on the head than reading the telephone book," and someone cuts me off and says, "Sensei, I think I know who stole the Buddha statue." Ah? Now that is interesting. Our large bronze Buddha statue was swiped a few weeks ago taken right off the altar and Yaku got us all worked up trying to catch the culprit, especially if it was an inside job. Well this guy is telling us he thinks he knows who did it and Yaku says, "Who, who?" and this guy – Tchang is his name – Tchang says: "Bombaclou!"

"Felix Bombaclou," the master repeats and squints his eyes. "Possible possible. Have you proof?"

Tchang gives his view of it, which isn't much, just hearsay, and no one pays him any further attention, they all just start talking again, talking talking, French people sure are a bunch of chatterboxes, and, as I say it's hard concentrating around this place I mean you would think you were in an Afghan carpet market not in a zendo, but I manage anyhow and hand back the pages. Voilà!

The place is emptying out, some people have jobs in this town I can see that, and Sensei and I go over a few of the items and he hands the pages over to Virginie for safe-keeping and puts his arm lightly over my shoulder and smiles and rubs his fingers together and says "You make any money yet?"

"No not yet" chuckle chuckle.

"What you do then, you continue to write?"

"Oh biensûr!"

"How many books you write?"

"Ah many I cannot count them anymore."

"And the only book you publish is my book *The Magic Fox*, yes?"

"Yes" I nod "but this time the book will be all mine" I point proudly to my chest "and the contract will be in my name too."

"Ah yes your name will be on it. But you must continue to write for me, for the Dharma, yes? You are a great religious writer."

"You think so?" Ha that's a good one! I know someone – a New York editor who, in fact, read some of these pages right here, and said I am only using Buddhism as a back-drop to write pornography.

"True," he pats me on the head, "I will give you some money you want some money?"

"Money? Sure."

"You come up to my room and I give you money."

"Okay" I nod "d'accord."

"But then you must not write pornography."

"Pornography?" I am surprised. What makes him think… "Well then Sensei how about I use another name? I make up a name, d'accord?"

"D'accord, d'accord…"

Just then the patient emissary from the embassy rises to his feet and coughs huun… huun… huun. Oh pardon says the master he had completely forgotten the old bloke. He signals for the emissary to approach and we are introduced, this is Michael Dalley the American boy, he writes splendid English he wrote *The Magic Fox*. Please Virginie get me a copy of the book.

Sensei and the emissary speak together in Japanese; they have completely forgotten me, now it's the emissary's turn; and when Virginie returns with the book, Sensei takes it and passes it on to the emissary. I get up and bid them off, with a respectful gassho, turn my back on them and look for the cashbox. Before I can get around to putting the four-franc soup-charge in the box, Arthur the money-collector calls me over. I don't much like being called over, especially when it has to do with money, I mean maybe he knows, maybe he saw me sneaking out the back yesterday. Mike, he says, don't forget to pay. / You think I was planning on skipping out? / Oh no, I just have to keep my eye on everybody. / What do you mean? / You know people sneaking out the back, things like that… I drop the four francs in the box, thinking he is on to me, and head out the door…

Order a coffee in the café. Arbalete and Nadia are here and they are happy to see me, they have been waiting for me in fact. Ah so, what's up? Well, they have several texts for the next issue of the *Zen News* and they want me to check them over. Man, all I wanted was to chew the breeze and look at the girls, and now this again. Is the stuff any good at least? I ask. Nadia shrugs and replies: They are well-known zen writers. / Okay okay, I say momentarily intrigued, Let's see the stuff. I start reading and right off I don't like it. A Ph.D. or something explaining the satori of the Sixth Patriarch. Now put that in your pipe and smoke it! Ah, here is something about the Buddha sitting for so long the grass grew tall all around his butt, not bad, I wonder if the grass tickled his balls, hehe, Hey man, let's have some beer. "A beer a page, okay?" "Okay," Arbalete toasts this agreement. It's a business deal, I dive into the task like any other editor, got the hang of it now, I get the beer like you get the money and I don't care what the man has to say about zen anymore, so long as the beer keeps flowing, I mean I kind of like reading the stuff, and I kind of like the author too, why if it wasn't for him... I drink down my beer and reach for another page.

We are standing at the counter and the job is finished and I am feeling okay when suddenly SHE shows up. We look at each other and I recall what happened last night. And so does she. But it doesn't matter, the past is the past and all that matters right now is she is looking directly into my eyes and I see us on a raft and the raft has split in half, that's how bad the storm was, and there is nothing to be done about it, the current is taking us to opposite ends of the earth never to be together again, never to know one another again; she is drifting from my life forever and ever it is the living death I tell you – I am swooning.

She is here somewhere, but I am not really sure where; can't see her, but I can smell her, I can feel her and frankly it's very hard to believe what's happening – me swooning? Well I am. Just like a woman. I am a woman and have always been one, machoness is just a game it's my trans-vestite act and for this at least I have no shame. In private away from prying eyes, in those moments of love-making I am actually rather tender, they all say it (sometimes). But this doesn't matter right now. I am holding onto the bar like it's the raft of life and I have just been knocked off, and I am all alone, it is cold down here and there is no one no one… Come on! I say to myself, Get yourself together! Nothing wrong with you man, you are just heartbroken, like every other bloke round here. Come on, act normal, offer the lady a drink. She is always good for a free drink. Excuse me but would you like a little drink, a cup of tea perhaps? No answer. I try again. Would you like a cup of tea, or a martini or a shot of Calva? No answer. Try again, Excuse me miss… Ah she's not even looking at me… I stare at the back of her head for a bit; just like in the café last night. Hmm she sure has a shiny pate today. Shaved her head has she? Ah the good little nun, atoning for her crimes, how nice… So I am looking at the back of her head which, when you think about it, is nothing compared to the front. Now the back, well frankly I never did like the back, something ugly and ignorant about it, something mean and tricky about that back part I do believe…

I am at Benoit Percheron's place. He is an iron-welder out of work or something and I am in his shower thinking it all over, first about myself and where I stand vis-à-vis the truth, I mean the true truth and I am thinking what a disap-pointment I must be to the master. The bad coin in the bunch, like my father used to tell me… That's right Yaku, call the ambulance; I have just bit the dust Yaku you can shovel me up and dump me in the trashcan now… But then one thing leads to the next, the mind being what it is for good or for bad, and I am recalling *that* night. My daughter and I were walking down the street that night minding our own business and who shows up in the cold black light, but HER. Kind of weird come to think of it, probably drunk, probably the booze giving her the courage to talk. Right on! A real honor! I mean it's the first words since we broke up and nice words at that, she invites us to the Café du Château for a drink, can you believe it. So I say Sure why not? and off we set for the Café du Château which is no château but the opposite, it's the hole of Calcutta. She orders a double Scotch and it's suddenly quite clear she is not going to be doing the paying, she did the inviting but this doesn't mean she is going to do the paying not the queen, but never mind my daughter slips me her pocket-money. Well we are standing there and she doesn't talk to me, doesn't answer my questions, nothing to say I guess, doesn't look at me either she is looking at some other guy and all I get is the fucking back of her head and there is nothing to look at there I know it by heart, know it almost as well as the front part, and I am getting a little angry but that's what she wants, to get me mad, she likes to see me fight – at least when it's for her – and so she is talking to this guy in a leather jacket with chains and things on it and I am just smoking my cigarette and drinking my drink – and hers too biensûr – and the next thing I know she is kissing the guy right on the mouth! My brain explodes or almost; I smother it sort of. And I look around the room, for nothing better to do, and I see my daughter she's playing the pinball machine. She is only ten or twelve and there is no one in this world means more to me, not even this bitch. In moments of explosion you need a counter-explosion and this is what happens, I have a good counter-blast, it crushes the whole show, I do not move; I am no one, but to the guy I am someone, to all his buddies I am someone, they know my connection, and the guy looks at me and we just look at one another nothing more, and it's like one of those stand-offs – will he move will he move? Well the guy steps back, like you do in karate, I've practiced it for years, and apparently so has he – one thing you never do is hang around too close – and my daughter pops up, Papa! You're not going to *fight* are you?

That does it. She pulls her guy out the door and it's over – the weepy story is over, and Celine (that's my daughter's name) and I are walking in the cold drizzle hand-in-hand and actually feeling okay.

4

I ran away from home with the circus,
Having fallen in love with Mademoiselle Estralada,
The lion tamer.
One time, having starved the lions
For more than a day,
I entered the cage and began to beat Brutus
And Leo and Gypsy,
Whereupon Brutus sprang upon me,
And killed me.
On entering these regions
I met a shadow who cursed me,
And said it served me right....

EDGAR LEE MASTERS

Didn't set the alarm for a change – on weekends zazen doesn't begin until 11, a good time to catch up on your sleep and to wake up as you will, like a pasha, but anyhow I wake up not as one will but rather in consequence of a natural need, and not at all naturally, no never naturally, either I get it in the brain with the alarm or in a bladder full of piss. Well, that's awakening for you, a brutal affair. Hunh what's that? Scritch-scratch scritch-scratch. Hey cut that out! I hit the side of the bed with my fist and almost piss on the sheets from the exertion. It's cold in here but my bladder is clamoring and I jump up and piss in the kitchen sink, light the stove for a little heat and inspect the mouse-trap. The bacon is still there – Oh! he got my spaghetti again went right through the cellophane... Cussing out the mouse and swearing I'm going to get him, I brush my teeth, comb my hair, shave, sprinkle on some aftershave and pull on a clean pair of pants, shirt, shoes – In a word I fix myself up good, it's Saturday at the dojo and there will be lots of people lots of old-timers new-timers, old ladies new ladies – and while I prepare myself, I count up my hours in bed six hours and forty minutes lulling in the sleeper's hospital, count up the time left me almost two hours with nothing much to do ah great, I sit down on the floor beside the untouched package of books, the package from the post office, take a sip of coffee light up a Camel, one of the five Caroline left behind for my convenience, rip open the package and lift out the top book, *Confessions* by Saint Augustine. Christian stuff. I flip through the pages, reading here and there, when something I read brings tears to my eyes. Don't know what, nothing to quote, no it's something between the lines, a kind of feeling, the saint-in-person perhaps, and I wipe my eyes and read more and the more I read the quicker my tears dry up, not so much from wisdom as from gloom, something about how Augustine once lived a life kind of like my own, but for him it was a wretched sinful existence, so departing from the crowd, from the likes of you and me, he stretched his hands to heaven and implored the people to baptize their children – because as everyone knows, we are all of us the very work of the Devil.

A priori I don't have anything against the Christian religion. I was raised and even baptized in it, into the Episcopalian church of course, but no one imposed it on me, except for the baptism part, and not much damage was done. At least not where good and evil is concerned. I mean

like they impose on most people we know, you know by
making them feel guilty and all that. Now, in Buddhism it's
a completely different story. In Buddhism you don't see
people going about doing nasty things to each other, like
nailing each other to crosses and shoving each other into
the fire and…, well it's another vision of life. Read the
Mahayana sutras and you travel between the planets going
through space and time at phenomenal speed and you go
back and forth too, and everywhere you go the place is
strewn with flowers and everyone you meet is a bodhisattva giving away all his money and stuff – no, not all!
he can't give all of it away because he has so much he can
never deplete his stock no matter what and…, ah it's getting late.

I wash the dried tears from my face, and bump down
the broken planks, and past the mailbox and, what's that, a
letter for me, my literary agent, good old Miss Robertson
and company, a fat check a contract a word of praise? Nope
just a note from the concierge. Wants to talk to me about all
that unpaid rent I bet.

The sun is nowhere and the sky is a grey sheet the color
of tin, like rain maybe. Turn right at the door pass some
guy reaching into a garbage can, turn left on the first corner, glimpse at the treetops showing over the wall of the
Montparnasse cemetery, leafless and as sad as you would
expect, continue down Losserand until I run into Natasha
going in the same direction. Did you see the new stamp on
the card? she asks. What stamp, what card? I ask. The
membership card! Membership card? You don't know? she

asks, in her soft surprised way, through her soft sensual body in her soft speaking seldom spoken voice, the product of a family of Marxist university professors, the parents having perhaps politicized themselves enough for their daughters for a lifetime, a good enough reason for sitting in meditation – at least it's quiet in the dojo – and she's been doing it even longer than me. I can remember those three years we sat side-by-side, on the right of the master, in front of our special tables, in the big plush dojo in the mountains, taking down the teaching, she into French and me into a kind of English straight from the horse's mouth, and now we are heading to the dojo together and she says, Everybody has a card, shows whether you're paid up, didn't Carmen give you one?

Well, it's like this, Carmen who runs the office, usually lets me in for free, but I don't tell Natasha, it's a secret; so I say, Oh sure, musta lost it.

Did you see the stamp they use, what do you think of it? / Can't remember, something special? / Here, look at mine… I look at it, a red-inked stamp of a monk laughing, Hotei or someone. The laughing beggar who lived in a burlap bag…

The dojo is packed, people piled on one another like in a burlap bag, it's the weekend crowd. Yakumatsu has become famous in the last years, especially on weekends, and if you don't get to the dojo well in advance you are not going to get a seat, it's just like going to the movies, and if you don't get a seat on the mezzanine, and you don't get one up on the gallery, nor behind the curtain in the gaitan, then you have to sit outside in the rain and cold, like some do… Laity and monks get no privileges around here and some have already given up coming on the weekends. Monks too can become indignant, what's this world coming to when a monk of ten years standing can't go to his temple anymore because the dingbats have taken over?

Sensei, certain monks keep telling him, you should get a bigger dojo. Just think, Sensei, how many more people you could have, and how much more money you would make off those cards with the laughing Buddha, haha. And we could find you a better apartment, a place where you can receive the celebrities, and why not? a fancy car with a shaved-headed chauffeur and…, and Sensei shrugs, what does he need with more disciples, says he, one disciple or even half a disciple, would do him fine. But Sensei, with a whole pile of mini-monks you can make a basket. You have a point, agrees the other. It's like during the Second World War, the master was right in the middle of it and whenever the Americans dropped their bombs, they would drop so many bombs, without even aiming, to hell with human life and all that; enough bombs and they would always hit the target, and sure, the master goes on, give the shiho, the transmission, to enough people and you will be bound to score a bull's-eye. Really? I ask the master, impressed by the simplicity of it all, recalling how Mahakashyapa got it by smiling at the Buddha one time on Vulture Peak and how the Sixth Patriarch got it by winning a poetry contest. Biensûr, replies the master, I will give the shiho to my top twenty disciples, and then here (the master gestures with his hand depicting a little explosion in space) paf! And there, paf!

Twenty minutes early and the dojo is full, not a seat left. Look at Georges Toutembrosse, whispers Ambrosio who is next to me, and I look at Toutembrosse, a monk of long-standing who goes plowing wildly into a corner cluttered with people dressed in jogging clothes and what not, pushing them round to make himself the regulation one meter times one meter-and-a-half sitting space, and Ambro and I laugh at the crudity of it all, and the kyosakuman by the door snaps out the house rules: No talking in the dojo!

Okay, okay, I take off my glasses and examine the lens before slipping them into my kolomo. Covered in dust, smudged with greasy fingers. I wipe them off on my long black sleeve wondering vaguely all the while why I never see this dust, this grease. I walk about with greasy vision and don't even know it.

Zazen begins and moments later the master arrives and, surrounded by his two female secretaries and the female inkin-ringer, he takes the honored seat.

...Having a hard time getting my breathing down... a good ten minutes go by... then suddenly I have got it, the breathing I mean; no, not the breathing, the posture, I mean the body, mind *and* breathing, all rolled in one, and just then Sensei starts talking, curiously, about the breathing. And, believe it or not, he is talking directly to me, to the exclusion of everyone else, funny isn't it?..., and he says people who are unhealthy cannot get their breathing down under their navels..., and now he is describing the breathing method, the secret one, the one practiced by all the ancient patriarchs, "If you learn this method and continue its practice, you will return to the normal condition (this is

Sensei's way of describing satori) for no one is in the normal condition. Americans too, they are not normal…"

I literally jump at this one. I am the only American in this place and…

"Michael Dalley brought me a present from America, a cigarette lighter on which is written 'I am normal'. In America people are not normal so they put this on their lighters." There is a pause, then: "Kyosaku!"

Kyo means stick and *saku* means wake up, and upon the master's command the kyosakumen go about waking up the people, whack! whack!... Now I know the different sounds, sometimes I can even tell who is on the stick just by the sound of the whack, like today, today you have Tchang the ex-Viet, and Emma Schweitzer the acupuncture doctor and… and what's that sound I hear? Pat-ta-THUNK! Pat-ta-THUNK! Yakumatsu himself is on the stick today! And he's going to get me for sure! Well, that's what happens, he picks me out of the bunch and gets me, with a double thunk! on each shoulder. And hard too.

But I like it – Now that it's over with. It's good for you, good for the concentration, cuts the bullshit sets you straight. And the harder the better. Now, the stick hasn't anything to do with sado-masochism or anything even remotely psychological, it has to do with how thick the skin is. The thicker the skin the harder you hit. Like hitting the horse, maybe you can't do the work for him but at least you can hit him.

By god, how long have I been sitting in this place?! Where am I?... I look around. Oooops, I'm in the dojo. Had forgotten. What time is it? Has he forgotten the time or what? Yaku never pays much attention to the clock, but God knows enough is enough. Enough wallpaper for today I do believe. I mean when a man's body-and-mind is geared to about one hour twenty, twenty-five and that hour twenty, twenty-five gets dragged over two hours, TWO HOURS, it's not the body that matters anymore, if you don't move an inch you enter another dimension, a place where you don't care about bodies and things anymore; it's the mind you begin to care about, because the mind is slowly going nuts. The brain – all of it, rational, irrational, the brain of the three worlds – is about to explode; it's like the brain is a sealed pot of shit and someone is holding it over the fire… I think about the others, going through the same thing. About the monks and the bodhisattvas and the new people in particular, sitting motionless for the first time in their colorful jogging clothes, and I imagine what is cooking in their own pots, knees above the boiling water, backs bent over, jawbones sagging and smoke everywhere, and it makes me laugh. All these good people boiling away in steaming pots of shit.

That's how Yaku runs this show, the more we number the more we sit. You might think that, under the circumstances, Yaku would make it easier, but not at all; it's a matter of quantity, the more we are, the more we sit. Clearly he's trying to get rid of us.

It's over, Yakumatsu has disappeared to his quarters in the facing building and many of us are milling about in the second dojo, round an improvised bar, coffee, tea or whiskey, and then I wander off, in a bum mood, don't like anybody. Here I am, in my Sunday best, and I feel out of it, an outsider unwanted and unwelcome, and spotting Benoit scowling in a corner I ask him: You got anything to smoke?... and we leave together.

Benoit is an unassertive low-key fellow, not much for socializing, but he likes to smoke, and we head over to his place, along the drizzly buzzing weekend street, along the lower part of Losserand, smelling of fish and garlic, and up to his place, an eight-floor walkup. Benoit once made love with my girlfriend, with HER and the whole thing went bad, particularly for Benoit, but that's all forgotten and we light up a joint and I talk to him about HER, who is still on my mind, and I will bet on Benoit's too, and he says she bewitched him or something, and I say sure, she bewitches everyone, and we go on talking about this and that, and I think of this fellow who is so different from me and with whom I get along so well. His father was a peasant or close to it, while mine was a rich man who resided in Monte Carlo, and Benoit was raised in a one-room farmhouse and he didn't even have a room of his own, let alone a bed, and he slept and lived in a corner. Me, I was born in what was once the Jimmy Walker mansion down on St. Luke's Place. Besides both of us having the same master, and the same girls, we also have our mothers in common. Both our mothers killed themselves when we turned eight, his by jumping into the farmhouse well and mine by gassing herself in the pantry. Well, things like this can make for an understanding which is there, without words.

Well I must leave off a package at the dojo restaurant. It's for Lartilleur (he is using my address for some stock dealings). The only hitch is that SHE works there as a waitress. I get to my feet, bid Benoit au revoir and head for the restaurant.

I walk in, ignore all the people and leave off the package. As I turn to leave, our eyes meet and she just looks back, blankly, as though at a vague shadow on the wall, and I say, for some stupid reason, I know it now, you never loved me…, and leave.

Ah well, we all say stupid things now-and-then, never mind. I am going to be rid of her very soon and that's all that matters. Get rid of her… I pass in front of the laundromat full of women, the butcher's shop full of meat and the music shop full of music. I stop to listen to the rock'n roll tune, roll myself a cigarette and stare up at the jittery city about me. Then head home.

That note from the concierge. It's still in my mailbox. I had hoped it would have flown away by now but it hasn't. Man, I just don't have the courage for this confrontation right now.

5

> One knows the hammer best when one uses it to hammer; and the nail, when one drives it into the wall; and the wall, when one drives the nail into it.
>
> HEIDEGGER

Today is Sunday and Celine slept over. There's only one bed and we share it – shared it ever since I left home some years ago. My wife and I split up when Celine was six so this means that today she is twelve, no thirteen, exactly thirteen, because today is her birthday.

Named after the French writer Louis-Ferdinand Céline. Céline the great genius of delirium (among other things) managed to make a bad name for himself as a jew-hater (among other things)… Now everyone knows a man can get away with almost anything these days, except of course that of being a jewhater. So the French people who have always loved and helped the Jews as history can prove, decided to execute him – Céline the writer I mean. But as nobody could get their hands on the man (he was in prison in Denmark during the hunt) the government confiscated everything he owned and took all his money, right down to his very copyright, and when four years later Céline was let out and returned to France he was besieged by journalists from all over. "Monsieur Céline" they asked him "what do you think of the Jews now?"

"Vive les juifs bon Dieu!" he replied.

Anyway when grandpa and grandma who are Jews, heavy into the Zionist movement, learned their granddaughter had been named after such a scurry rat…, well they took it badly.

I tried my best to soothe feelings as you can imagine, but what can you say, you can't go around apologizing for the name you gave your daughter, so I said: Look, I gave your granddaughter this name in thanks to the writer, to what he wrote, not to the man, not to what he did or didn't do. It was "Thankyou for *The Voyage to the End of the Night*, thankyou for *Death on the Installment Plan*," that's all.

Frankly I can't take this kind of problem seriously. To me it's a lot of bull. I mean what the man did or didn't do and all that. That's in another department, like down in the basement or somewhere. And what's more, when you think of it, who says his book, or any books, are so great anyhow? Céline, Rabelais, the Bible and the sutras, they – them – are just words, just writing. How did Yaku put it? About writing in the long run being useless or something…?

I ooze out of bed before the alarm goes off, creep into the kitchen and inspect the mousetrap. The bacon is still intact but he got into the spaghetti again. I prepare the breakfast a cup of tea and a piece of bread for Celine a cup of coffee and a cigarette for myself. Then I wake her up, happy birthday to you etc. and give her a present, a chess set, it's in the style of a leather attaché-case and it makes her dapper in her roller skates.

We walk down the same old street, she to the subway and me to the dojo, and we are at the curb in front of the café Le Métro and Jean-Paul Beauneveu is standing in the doorway, it's not yet 11 am and he's drinking beer the mug of which he holds up to us in greeting. I call out to him that if he wants some clothes to come by my place. I have some more stuff.

Why do you always give clothes to JP? / Cause JP is the poorest guy in the dojo he's got nothing. / He's even poorer than you papa? / That guy doesn't even have a pot to piss in. / He has no home? Where does he sleep? / He sleeps here and there and sometimes in the dojo I guess. / He doesn't work, either?

I look down at my daughter. We are holding hands. "You mean for money? For money he makes it emptying garbage cans in some of the buildings on the block."

We are standing in front of the subway entrance, Celine is going back to her mother and it's good-bye time. Perhaps she will be sleeping over again next weekend, perhaps not. I kiss her good-bye and watch her hop down into the underground, her new chess set under her arm. I feel a pang somewhere inside, seeing her off like this is not normal, we will miss one another.

Today is Sunday and there are even more people on Sundays than on Saturdays and you have to move even faster for a seat and so here we are, sitting smack in the aisle, back pressed up against the altar, knee sticking into the ribs of the pottery man, Hey Leponte, can you move forward a bit? / Hey, you over there, move up will you?

Once we are all squeezed but comfy into position, unable to move either to the left or to the right for fear of losing an inch to a neighbor, I stare in front of me. At the back of Leponte's shaved head. Lots of people shave their heads around here. It's part of being a monk, the part I don't like. Has to do with detachment but myself I like my hair too much obviously. Not the hair itself, no one cares about hair itself, no it's the hat part of hair I like. And then there's Montparnasse, the Sélect, the Coupole. You know how they talk at the Coupole? "Dear me," says a lady "look at that fellow – he lost all his hair!" "No my dear" replies a gentleman, "he is one of those Hara Krishna fruitcakes."

Someone pinches me, it's Sophie. Like myself, she is wearing her hair-hat and black kimono, and it is a good thing – to wear the kimono I mean – particularly here in the dojo, hides those healthy young buttocks and the large full tits. Couldn't handle it otherwise. So Sophie pinches me and my mind's eye pierces through her kimono like a laser beam – don't know why, I didn't will it to happen it just happened – and I see it all, just like God made her, and damn it my cock actually twitches! No kidding. In fact my cock, which I had carefully deposited on top of my left thigh and against my belly, goes and jumps right out of its place, and now I must reach under my kolomo, pick it up and put it back where it belongs. These girls are little devils in disguise they are.

Was the whiskey any good? Sophie whispers. Oh yes the whiskey. Sophie works as a cashier in one of the local supermarkets and a few days ago I walked away with three shopping bags full of drinkables and eatables, and all free of charge too, thanks to the cashier standing over me here in the nude.

Twelve minutes more before the bell, twelve minutes more and already people are being turned down at the door. Through the big bay windows in front of us three rows up, we can see the shadows of the disgruntled walking off. Ha, there goes Georges Toutembrosse, didn't get a seat today. He who has been here since the beginning and was ordained a monk years and years ago has been turned down at the door. It wasn't like this before was it Georges? Well times have changed, this zen master is à la mode nowadays.

The air is very heavy in the dojo, comes from outside, look at it out there, neither sky nor sun, only a leady greyness which seeps in everywhere… I gaze at the view before me, not so lovely, not like you would expect of a Buddhist zendo, not like in America not like in Japan, no pine groves no lawns not even a rock garden, just the second dojo that fat squat concrete block a bunkerhouse, a couple motor bikes parked on the pavement a pavement stained with splotches of oil and grease, and one tree a puny little thing sticking out of some greenish slime. That tree has always caught my eye, for years now I have been looking at that tree and it never seems to grow despite what some of these religio-mystical types around here say about it. See that tree, it's just sparkling with life! And you know why, why because it's located directly between the two temples, it's in the crossfire of good zazen vibes. That's what they say, but I think it's croaking.

Everybody crosses his legs in the posture and the kyosakuman hits the gong ten times and the sound resounds through the dojo, the courtyard and over a good part of the neighborhood. The bank clerk at the BNP across the street once told me he always hears the twelve-thirty bong for zazen. It's the signal for lunchbreak at the bank... And for that tenant in the building across the yard, for him the gong is the signal for the beginning of Mass. Every Sunday and directly after the gong has been struck, that tenant flings open his window and blasts us with some Christian hymns, things like *Onward Christian Soldiers*, over his stereo. He has a point to make and we all get it. Lately, however, he appears to have grown tired listening to his own crap. Today he's playing organ music, and it's very cozy in the dojo right now, whatwith the raindrops falling on the skylight and the organ notes. Why it's J.-S. Bach I do believe... Don't know how much time has elapsed, there is no kyosaku, the master is not talking and Bach flows in between the raindrops and it's all very quiet... No way of knowing how much time has passed, a short time a long time it's all the same, and now the master is talking and I tune in to hear him say he wants these kusens, these teachings he is now giving on the *Shinjin Gakudo* to be corrected by Michael Dalley.

Usually Yaku doesn't mention me, usually he mentions Dagoba or Lamponéon or Peppone or somebody. But now he's onto my case. Yaku needs me now, now that I have copped out. Work is piling up and someone must do it and seeing that the teaching is in English and seeing that I am the only anglophone in this sangha, me and Lee that is, and seeing that I already did one book for him, *The Magic Fox*, and have finished the draft of a second one tentatively called *In the Balls of the Dragon*, it's only normal that my quitting at this point deserves some attention. But me I have other things on my mind right now and it's not his work either but mine. I mean everyone knows there is no cash to be made in sutra work. Me I have something in the oven, and it's going to make money you will see. It's a story, about my Monte Carlo days, my cool old dad, his wife the sexiest little bitch you ever saw, and their friends Onassis, Ali Khan and Rita Hayworth – all that salable stuff and written from the inside – and it's going to sell like hotcakes. The manuscript is with my agent in New York and there will be a contract any day now and a quick trip to New York compliments of the publishers and there will be lots of rewriting and all. So just hold on Yaku, once the contracts are signed and the rent is all paid and my daughter's schoolbooks taken care of, then I will devote myself entirely to you, once I have money, Yaku, I will do zazen all the time and serve you as a disciple should.

"To study the way is to practice with body and mind" says the master "to study the way is to study the self and to study the self is to forget the self and to forget the self is to be one with all existences everywhere…"

You know, the first time I heard this phrase "to study the self is to forget the self" etc., I almost cried. That's how hard it hit me. But this was a long time ago and now it doesn't touch me one bit. It's become another cliché. Christianized and sodomized and all that's left of it, at least for me, is that last little word still unleveled, the word 'everywhere'. "...And to forget the self is to be one with all existences everywhere." Everywhere? even on Pluto on Saturn in other galaxies in heaven and in hell, become one with God and one with the Devil?... "Practice and satori are two sides of a piece of paper, says the master, look at one side and you can't see the other, so unity..."

Leponte is uncrossing his legs; he's got rheumatism of the joints like me but me I am not moving not yet not yet but any moment now, no, not now, now? nono, now? nono, what the –?

The kyosakuman is messing with my body. Shoving his knee in my back. Pulling on my head. Okay okay, but lay off will you? It's alright to correct the postures, that's your job, but not *now*! Not when we are in the last stretch jackass! I mean it's like correcting the marathon runner heading into Athens –

"There are no relatives and no opposites here and one side of the paper never thinks he should be the other side, so it is with self and other with self and society self and the cosmos."

Jackass is still at it. There I was heading into the cosmos and thanks to Jackass I'm boiling away in a steaming pot of shit. Easy boy easy. Listen to the teaching.

"...There is nothing impure no impurity exists between the sides, impurity is the Devil, originally there is no Devil between God, Buddha and self."

Hunh? No Devil between? Must be his bad English doesn't know what he is saying anymore. Haha even the translator is stumped, go ahead say something say anything it doesn't matter anymore we're all boiled dry... Well it's René Manivel translating and he doesn't translate it he just waits for the master to repeat himself but the master goes right on, he's forgotten the translator, forgotten us, forgotten everything.

"...We must not look at the right from the left, one-sided views lead to opposition relativity and contradiction as between self and other man and woman classes races countries, people separate and there is war."

This brings HER to mind – I mean maybe she and I should never have separated, what a bloody mess she hasn't spoken to me in a kalpa or two.

"...This is only a continuation of barbarism, a new civilization must now arise a civilization of peace..."

Off with the kesas and the rakusus and the black robes and the white robes underneath the black ones and into jeans, fur coats and street shoes. The bar is working well – the dojo bar – and everyone is here, Yaku in the back and SHE up front. I sure could use a drink but no one's offering and I just stand round doing nothing in my jacket, jeans and cowboy boots with the patched hole up front (the boots were a gift from my brother Peter years back in Wyoming) just watching HER and Ambrosio talking up a storm and Yaku sitting quietly in a corner and looking splendid in his monk robe and wooden sandals, and I watch him watch the people, never seen Yaku looking so timid before. Ah now he is smiling up at someone and to someone else he nods and shakes hands with him and now he is laughing (this someone probably just told Yaku a joke) and he has the laughiest head of pliable leather you have ever creased.

There is no point in standing around with your teeth hanging out your mouth man. Go over and talk to him or take a walk or something. Easily said, I am magnetized to the spot, can't approach him any closer can't move off too far either, a question of heat and each has his own threshold in this matter and me I am really what you might call the lukewarm type, you know likes it neither too hot nor too cold but just right, that is around 20 degrees centigrade.

Well, I manage to get my lukewarm blood to circulate again and now we are talking anyway. The teaching was very good today Sensei, thankyou. I bow. He reaches into the sleeve of his kolomo searching for something, probably the text, and quickly I assume a grave expression and tell him how busy I am these days. I am a year behind on the rent, I actually tell him, And what about Stanley, can't he do it in my place, he's American.

Yaku takes three quick puffs on his cigarette, puts it out in an ashtray produced by Viviane, out of nowhere, rises to his feet, turns his back on me and leaves.

I know, I am heartless. My heart is elsewhere… I catch sight of HER, catch a last glance of her catching a last glance of me, and all I can feel is the longing, to go to her, to rest my weepy head on her lap; but I walk out instead, into a world full of dogs' excrement and other muck, and head home.

Always amazes me, how can a person be so cut in two, be so two-faced, how is it a man can follow say the Way of Buddha and at the same time be such a…

I drop the whole thing, suddenly, somehow. Stretch the backbone, pull in the chin…

Today I am going to do something constructive, going to see the concierge, talk to her about the rent, yes I am always putting off reckoning and this just won't do. So I am standing with my finger on the concierge's doorbell, about to push it in, when suddenly it occurs to me that today is Sunday and it is not nice to disturb people on Sunday especially when it's to do with unpaid bills not about to be paid just sweet-talked, and sure, it occurs to me that Louise and Emile, the wife-and-husband are on their day off and of course their boy who is in the army now and probably home on furlough are all about to sit down to their Sunday dinner, and dropping my hand from the bell, I head along the dim hallway full of lunchtime odors and, head bent, I walk up to my room on the top floor.

Take care not to push the door too hard, it's a real rotten door and this wouldn't be the first time it has fallen off its hinges, so in it swings ever so softly and – the mouse! There he goes! Quick, in the kitchen! I dash into the kitchen, but he's gone, vanished. And the trap is still there, the bacon untouched. But the spaghetti that's another matter. Maybe he doesn't like bacon, maybe he only likes spaghetti. Okay get out of the spaghetti you, I am cooking up what's left.

There's a knock on the door. I shovel in the last of the spaghetti, you never know who might be behind that door, take the spaghetti right back out of my mouth or something, and shout mouth full, Come in! Come in!

Well well it's Jean-Paul Beauneveu, come for the clothes. He's looking unusually dapper, got that affluent plump air about him today.

I see you're eating at any rate, I joke with him, or is it just the booze?... Jean-Paul's big problem is he drinks too much, and because he drinks too much he doesn't get laid enough. The thing is all his earnings from collecting garbage go into the booze and the ladies won't have anything to do with him, it would cost them too much money.

Both! he gives me a toothy-gapped smile and goes on to tell me, and very happy about it all, that he has a real job now. He pulls his ear, his good one – his other ear is only half there, the other half he lost in a traffic accident – and tells me that he is a chauffeur nowadays. The car is parked downstairs. It's a limousine, a lee-mooo-zeeen, you wanna see it?

Christ I know what a limousine looks like, hell man I was born in one.

You're sure? Come on, I'll show it to you.

Ah JP wants me to see the limousine not because it's a limousine, but because he's telling the truth for a change, no bullshit this time he's really got a job and he wants to prove it... Hey, how much did you make when you were emptying garbage cans? / Fifty francs a day. / How long does it take to empty them? / About half-an-hour. / How many buildings you gotta look after? Two, three?... Say, that's not so bad, I think, I could do that myself.

I give him the clothes, shove them in a plastic bag, a pair of grey flannels and a couple of cowboy shirts, perfect

74

stuff for the job. Hey, I call after him on the landing, good luck on your new job and don't lose the other ear you hear.

Phone is ringing. My wife. You know, Michael, it's your daughter's birthday today and I guess you never thought about giving her a birthday party yourself, it's too much trouble for you but it doesn't matter because Frederique has organized a party at her place, they've gone to a lot of trouble, buying a cake and drinks and inviting friends and of course you're invited too and perhaps it would be a nice thing to bring some flowers, you can afford some flowers can't you? We should be at her place in about an hour, so see you then.

So here we are, going from moment to moment, from life to life, at Fred's and Didier's place, Fred is my niece, that is my late sister's daughter, a six-foot blonde, a stunning creature, happy, friendly and intelligent – everybody agrees to this – she was first in school, first at the university and now she's a child psychoanalyst and she's first in this too. Didier is her husband, they have known one another since they were kids and they got married on Fred's eighteenth birthday. He's tall, about six-foot-four and he has just embarked on a career as a businessman and his prospects are very promising, he is alert and enterprising and as a husband he is thoughtful and loving. In fact they are a happy and striking couple and they radiate together the finest of feelings. But what matters to them doesn't matter to me. Anyhow, at least I know where they live, the street number, phone number and even what clubs they belong to and how they handle their finances – this is more than they know about me their only uncle Dalley I can tell you… Anyway they have one handsome child of four with another on the way, and they have lots of friends too, all from good families, and some of them are here today and I can't see them as other than wallpaper, no matter how hard I try… The truth is they snub me. I got myself disinherited. I don't belong, I'm socially unfit and all that, and what the hell who cares, I mean what has Fred done with her life that makes her so great I ask you, besides planning things – their nuptials, their house in the country, their old age – living just that, all the way right to the coffin. I mean after all they – she – should show some interest in good old uncle Dalley bravest of the brave, I mean I could show them a thing or two about life and whatnot, they are still kids and haven't yet done diddle. But hell with all this self-praise who am I to think such things, I mean today is my daughter's 13th birthday and she is sitting on my lap because there are no other kids around to play with, and my niece is serving up the hot chocolate and my nephew, that is my late sister's son, is talking to me and, no, he's not into nuptials or anything like that, not him, he is round-headed with a face about as smooth as the outside of a pineapple, what I mean is his at least is no run-of-the-mill beauty face, and what's more when his father dies he will become the Count de Something, from a fine old family indeed. Well, despite his strange appearance, my nephew is impeccably dressed and, though only in his early twenties he carries himself like an old decrepit gentleman. Also he is sharp-witted and quick and can tie anybody into knots, and yet the funny thing is he has failed all his exams from A to Z and doesn't have a job, can't find one because oddly enough no one will hire him. Anyway, he is now telling me about the last time he threw a bomb in a bookstore (he belongs to some kind of rightist organization, not to mention to the un-Buddhist-like rightist Nichiren sect) and next he tells me about meat-eaters. He is a diehard vegetarian and he enjoys making mincemeat out of Buddhist meat-eaters, and what the hell he wants to get me so bad, I let him have me. Save the animals and shoot me dead!... While my nephew rants and raves the Nichiren doctrine in my ear I wink at a well-bred little lady with large feet on the sofa…, Jesus where's the liquor, Oh yeah hi man, I greet my half-brother, no point in getting into him now, suffice it to say that my half-brother at least didn't get disinherited, which means he doesn't do much of anything, doesn't have to, he's got everything, his name is Winnifred Junior and he has a swanky flat in the right neighborhood and money galore. Anyway, Winnifred and I get along, I mean you can't hold one's karma against a man can you, and we get to talking about coke and dope and about his latest deal (he deals as a pastime) with the local dealer (none other than my wife's lover Roger) and lo-and-behold if it isn't my wife come over with a cup of hot chocolate. Hey where's the hard stuff? lots of chocolates and crumpets but where's the hard stuff?...

Here comes Didier, husband and host. Grand to be here. / Grand to have you, replies he and we shake hands and smile. He's another guy I kind of like, despite my bad mood, despite his handsome face, despite everything. I ask him a few polite questions concerning his latest business venture (something to do with real estate) and he does likewise. Are you still writing? Are you still following that zen master? (I notice nobody in our family ever asks me how I make ends meet – it's only pleasant stuff we talk around here). Yes, biensûr, I reply… The exchange would have ended here had not my wife cut in: Michael, tell Didier about the book you got published… So I tell him… Is it selling well? / Yes yes oh no the book isn't selling at all. / I am sorry to hear that. / Yes me too. The publishers burned all the copies no kidding. / No kidding? Why is that? / It's a long story. The American zen community over there sabotaged it… I am about to tell the story but Didier isn't interested and he cuts me off and says: Tell me, you did make *some* money on it didn't you? / Well yes a little, not more'n this though. / How much is that? / Oh that? Not much. You see Didier, I gave the copyright away. / You did? To whom? / To the master.

This stops him from asking the next question, like for instance, How do you make ends meet then? and having little left to say, Didier moves on and now we are alone me and my wife.

I am telling my wife, what I want right now is a drink, and my wife is telling me in turn, this is a kid's party and Fred has decided she's going to keep it this way, a kid's party. / Yeah? I look under the chair, then where are all the kids I don't see'em… A big help she is. I get up and look behind the bar. The bottle-rack is empty empty! Hey what's this crap? I say. / I told you the party is for your daughter, she whispers and don't speak so loud. / I mean *ba*bee, they went and hid all the bottles they *hid* them! Now why'd they go and do that, cause of me? / No it's just that you get so awful when you're drunk. / I wouldn't get *drunk* what's wrong with you? / Besides you're on an empty stomach, you'll be groveling on the floor before you even – / Whadya mean *groveling*?

What are you two whispering about? cuts in the stupid little thing with the rich lovely big feet on the sofa. Oh we are simply chatting away. A wonderful party this is don't you think? With all the booze and all yes? And what do you do in life ma belle, oh no kidding me too, I don't do anything just hang round with my mouth open sponging off the good people you know…

Ooops time to finish with this little chat, par'n me ma'am it just shat out on it's own nothing to do with me.

Keep the dignity what. I pour myself a cup of hot chocolate get to my feet and stare out the window at the Paris rooftops. After a moment's pleasure looking at the Paris rooftops I think of my wife Lydia and her latest insult. *Me groveling on the floor*, she must be kidding what's more I am *not* on an empty stomach, why does she always pick on me, why does everybody always pick on me I wonder. I sit back down, blow away the steam rising from my cup which is like my brain and sip the hot choco- late. And all the while I repeat my mantra to myself, Keep the dignity man, keep the dignity man, keep the…

Everyone is talking except me and since I am not even listening (my thoughts are on my next move, getting out of here before I wreck it, me and the party that is) and I get up to bid my good-byes. But Lydia doesn't want me to leave. It would be rude, she says. / Rude hell, I've already been here an hour. / Look around you Michael, this is your daughter's party and Fred has been very kind to do this for us and after all you are Celine's father and you are Fred's uncle!

Yeah that's my big problem. I have eyes and all the rest too and all they see is my family and my senses all want the same thing. All of us to hold hands and commiserate, but this being quite impossible, being that I don't belong and all that, not even to my own family, all I want now is to run, get away from it, from my problem from my family, or what's left of it. I tell you it's a spider-web made out of rope and it's choking me, me who is father and uncle to them all in my own right, strangled to death on the livingroom floor… Anyway, I fight down the old recollections and say to Lydia, Okay I'll stay for another half hour. But not a minute more mind you!

Twenty-five minutes later I jump up, grab my jacket with the torn-up sleeve and bid them all good-bye. Good-bye Didier, good-bye Fred, I say to my niece with the bulging belly, Nice talking to you haha-hehe-ehe, and head for the door.

I am almost out when Lydia catches up with me on the landing: Can we get together this evening? / No not tonight, tonight Caroline's coming over. / But I thought you said that tonight… / Tonight I'm busy, I reply and it's true too, Caroline is coming over. / That girl? That's not fair! I had it all arranged, tonight Celine is staying over at Fred's and I thought we could talk – / Talk? Talk about what? Talk about that guy Roger Whatshisname you've got at home, we could talk about him waiting for you with his dick in his hand, waiting for you while we talk – wait for Mr. and Mrs. Dalley while they talk!…

Lydia grabs my jacket zipper in her fist and says pleading, Just for a little while. / Oooh, *okay*! but just for a little while.

It's not much later and I haven't had a minute to myself all day and I am going slowly nuts – keep the dignity man, keep the dignity – and Lydia is present again, present in a new decor but present anyhow, and we are both sitting opposite one another, me on the bed she on the chair, and I am drinking wine and she is drinking water and we talk about our up-coming divorce case. She says she doesn't want to get divorced and I am saying the opposite –

– Look I want that divorce!

– Well I'm not going to sign so there!

– I don't want to talk about the divorce anymore if that's okay with you.

– Then what do you want to talk about?

– I don't want to talk about anything.

– Then what do you want to do?

– Look I've got work to do. So why don't you leave okay?

– No I won't leave not until we're friends again.

– Sure we're friends (says I, doubtfully). You know what you mean to me.

– Oh I don't just mean "friends".

– Oh that. (I look at my watch.) Look I've got a date.

– Yes and you had a date with me too!

I scratch my head trying to remember and at the same moment catch a glimpse of myself in the full-length mirror looking like the local idiot, but had I really made a date with her too? idiot or not I don't know. Anyway I have my arms around her narrow waist and her 3-inch breasts are pressing against my chest and I am kissing her, a kind of good-bye kiss or something and she reaches for my balls and says: Let's make love. Nono. I think of Caroline who will be by shortly and of my work which is waiting, maybe if she would sit quietly over in the corner for a bit we could get some writing done around this place maybe huh? huh? and with that I turn to open my typewriter and start writing. I am writing a bit about Buddhism when Lydia pops up out of the blue and sits smack on my lap and starts kissing me. What's wrong with you, she wants to know, Come kiss me on the lips. What's wrong with *you*, says I, opening my knees and dropping her to the floor, haha. Now she's up again and she's got me by the neck, it may just be a loving embrace but to me it feels like the wife's got me in a stranglehold and I struggle frantically to free myself, it's a struggle which has been going on for years, and the whole thing is getting out of hand and I break free and rush to the door and fling it open, You've got to go!... Well, Lydia starts to cry. The tears run down her face bringing the mascara eyelashes and cheekbones along with it, which touches me – what was it Yaku said this morning? to forget the self is to be one with everyone – and so I say, Okay okay, and close the door.

We start talking again. The tone has changed, more heartfelt you might say, and Lydia says she wants me back because she loves me and because she is frightened of a life without me, and after all these years together it's understandable enough. I feel the same. But then again things which appear simple enough on the surface can be very complicated underneath, for instance there's this problem of money or rather of lack of money – it's her problem really, she's scared of finding herself in the street if things were left to me, but of course this is a lot of hogwash. Money of course is never an obstacle, unless you make it one. For me the problem is more immediate, it has to do with her boyfriend Roger – Roger the Lodger – you know the guy who lives at my place, in my place, or what was once my place, moved in lock-stock-and-barrel he has, and well Lydia kind of likes it, in some strange way, and what the hell, it's just too damn late, the parts don't fit like before, like before when there was no Yakumatsu no zen and no lodgers… Ah the whole thing is one huge pain in the ass, can't we talk about something else, about the dojo for instance, sure that would make me feel better – but she doesn't want to talk about the dojo, that's the last thing which interests her, like I said the parts just don't fit anymore, there is no way of talking anymore, we have used it all up, so let's just sit quietly and take it easy okay…

The phone rings. Hello Liz? (Liz is Jackson's girl, my good friend Jackson isn't doing too well, he has cirrhosis of the liver and his chances are poor) and Liz is giving me the latest news but you can hardly hear her voice, it's as soft as a mouse, and I must press both ear-pieces to either side of the head to get the message. Where is he now? I ask. / He's back home. / I thought he was in the hospital… Well it seems when Jackson woke up and found himself in a hospital – the American Hospital over in Neuilly – he punched the nurse in the nose and hit the doctor with a chair, on his way out. Jackson is hooked on wine and he drinks the cheapest rot and when the doctors tell him he must cut out the drinking, he answers that it's his own fucking life and he doesn't need their brilliant diagnosis to save him, in fact he hates their guts, and well he is back at the house and he would like to see you Michael when you have a moment. He's in awful pain.

I hang up and pour myself a glass of wine, a big one for Jackson, and damn if we don't get into an argument about wine drinking, Lydia is comparing me to Jackson and she gives a rundown on all the evils of drinking, just like the doctor; and myself, acting like Jackson, I get to my feet ready to punch her, just like Jackson did to the doctor – I am Jackson suddenly and I admire his last act – and Lydia and I go at each other like cocks in a courtyard.

What I mean is here's a man dying, and all it does is make things worse, instead of better as you would think it might.

Okay you've gotta go! I shout, ripping open the door and staring menacingly at her, Now GO!

My eyes see sparks and flashes my ears hear the screams in a no exit sanatorium; Lydia's face is full of hate and hate breeds hate and all I want is to hit out at it, murder it myself before it murders me but I sort of control myself, and she is saying something about the divorce again and that she will sign it all right, And you, she spits out, You dirty drunken wino can go to hell! and off she stomps hitting the wooden-planked steps hard with her boots, and I cuss her out myself and slam the door. I fling it open again, about to shout another insult at her when Jeanine the neighbor, old stinkbag, opens her own door and her turd-colored dog barks insanely at me and I am about to kick that damn turd in the jaw when a whiff of human stench and dogshit hit me in the olfactory glands and all I am thinking of now is of closing my door fast, before the smell –. I slam the door again.

Or try to, but the door hits the threshold on a slant and a splinter of wood and a broken hinge-screw hit the floor, and I stare at the fucking door which has just fallen off its hinge, and the thing looks so stupid so funny stupid, like a wino hanging by an arm in a doorway, a picture so far removed from the moment and yet somehow so close to it, that it makes me laugh, Oh Jackson you old sonofabitch.

The door. Now what? Well, it's got to be fixed and quickly too, before Stinkbag across the way finishes me off. I throw open the window, let the cleansing air of a cold twilight take over, pick up a hammer and a nail, one of my two hammers and one of my many nails, the smaller hammer and the rightsized nail, and I slap the hammer in my hand. Now I am busy with the door, and knowing the virtues of doing something, I concentrate on the hammer and then on the nail and then on the door. Now I take up a wrench and tighten the loose bolts in my brain, for I tell you my concern goes further than the door, further than the stench, further than my wife and all that hell, or perhaps not so very far at all, it's always hard to tell where the problems really lie, it's hard to find the root of things, nevertheless I concern myself with the door. No not just the door, the hammer the nail and the door.

Now that the door is back in place and I have nothing more to do, I think of Lydia again and the whole rigmarole starts all over. Oh mama. The short life of Mr. Satori. It's like the marathon runner in the last stretch, no time to think, no-mind, clear as crystal; but the limited law only lasts while you work; once night has fallen and the day's work is over, you are back where you started, grappling away among a pack of shadows.

I heat up some coffee roll a cigarette and read a little Huang-po, taking it in like you would a pill, a full bottle, a kill or cure remedy, a kind of transfusion, a potion, a salve, an ointment, a quick little bit of psychotherapy, waiting for the phenomena to settle as they say like sediment at the bottom of a wine bottle – but nothing is settled and I throw the book aside, glance at my watch and think of Caroline. She should be here in a while and darn it I don't want to see her. Don't want to see anyone. Just to be alone, like a good monk should, with an empty head, without women without anything… Well Huang-po didn't work either. Once upon a time books like this, you know transcendental stuff, could do the trick. But now nothing works. Maybe it's zazen which precipitated all this, I dunno. Makes you see the futility of things… Maybe I'll do a little zazen. Why not. Better to do things, not just talk about it, fix the door, put on your rakusu and sit on a cushion…

When I come out of it some time later I think: Let's get this day together, or what's left of it. Do some work, a little writing or something. What's the time? Oh I forgot, Caroline! Well that's okay, that's just fine. After all, like they say in zen, everyday is a good day, and if a little cha-cha-cha is in store right now, then why not. Besides it's good for the muscle tone, a tonic for the body, a bolster to the morale and a renaissance for the brain. So let's see, says I feeling for my cock and balls to see if they're still there, what we should do right now is prepare ourselves for the visit, sweep the rug, clean the glasses, clean the genitals, brush the teeth, shave the face, change the underpants, and the overpants too, the tight corduroy ones bought and cut to fit by Chevalier my mentor, and that loose-fitting shirt comes from –. Let's see, fifteen minutes to go, keep the interest going, think about your cock, think about her… I pick up a dirty book about a chambermaid and her master Mr. Dalley and I am on the bed reading away and my o my the things Mr. Dilly-Dalley does to Caroline his chambermaid, she's the most sensual bitch in heat you have read off a page and Dilly-Dalley has her suck off all the guests and then he calls in horny old JP Beauneveu the chauffeur who takes her doggie-style on the Persian rug…

There is the softest most delicious knock on a broken door you have ever heard, the sweetness of which – Oh happy day, she has arrived!

The lady is wearing the soft fur coat and the in-style high black boots, and I rub my hands together – figuratively speaking of course – and think, Now I'll show you sweetheart how a real man handles it you bet. I stop her in the middle of the room right in the line of the butagaz, open her coat and take a look. Madame is wearing my favorite color, a long tightish woolen azure-blue dress through which you can see the garterline. Hunh, first time she's ever worn a garterstrap, ah she's a hot little bitch I can tell – I mean my cock immediately curves up to her like a cucumber, and well sure it's hidden in my pants but she knows it, knows how it works, and while my hands caress her waist and hips, she presses close and buries her head in my neck and starts nibbling…

We are in bed and my fingers seek out the prominent bumps under her thick head of hair and for a second I think of *her*, of how I used to lick her skull (when it was clean-shaven), and her head rests in the pit of my shoulder and she tells me her problems, her ex-husband attacking her in court for child-kidnapping and quickly I am asleep.

I am awoken by the ring of the phone. It's Felix Bomba-clou. Hurry! Hurry! he shouts over the receiver, you've got to come to the Sélect it's important! / Jesus Christ, what time is it? / You must help me, Il faut que tu m'aides! pleads Bombaclou. I tell you they're going to get me! / Hunh? What's going on? I ask getting out of bed and glancing over at my clothes. What's cooking man? / It's going to be bad, the head guy's using a silencer! / A silencer? Look man, I don't want to get shot, I just want to sleep. / Listen, they're five of 'em and – / Hey, Felix, can't you find someone else to help – ? / You're the only guy who can help me! and too you live next door! Now please! Hurry! hurry! / Felix, I say suddenly remembering how crazy he is, Felix tell me a bit about it first, I mean who are these guys? / I told you! It's the KGB, they're after me!

Yes sure, I hang up, clack… Clack! Clack! What's that? Came from the kitchen. The mousetrap! I got the mouse.

6

Those who think they must work to earn a salary are poor fellows, and those who study in order to earn money afterwards are hopeless.

MADAWAKI

Monday is hosan, day-off for the monks, an ancient tradition. So thanks to the ancient tradition I can loaf around in bed today. Sure is great, not rattled awake by an alarm clock, wake up when you want, get up when you want. Oh-hum what time is it? 9 am, what are you doing Caroline? Getting dressed. Acting like she has a job or something. Where are you going? Oh it's for the kid. The kid is at C.'s parents' house over in Antony in the banlieu and he's waiting for her. She is scheduled to take him to school on Monday, the father on Tuesday. Well she's late, the kid won't get to school until around 11 and the father who's to pick him up after school every Monday (she picks him up on Tuesday) will tell it to the judge. On Monday February 13th of this year your honor my boy was three-and-a-half hours late for school, the mother was late because she spent the previous night sleeping with a certain Monsieur Dalley on whom my lawyer has a file – worked in the pornography business, presently unemployed, two police records, an adherent to an un-Christian mystical sect...

So the jerk has built up a file on his ex-wife's propria persona and already I figure in it somewhere.

Oh thankyou sweetheart, coffee in bed how thoughtful of you... Yep it's great to have a woman...

The woman is gone and I am in bed propped up against the moist wall of cheap mortar thinking of the day before me only waiting for to be filled by cosmic activity and, let's see, what's on the agenda for today? A good time to answer some letters. Maddux in Asheville, Heidi in Hamburg, Robertson in Manhattan. Robertson is my literary agent, a very fine one, and sexy too. She's about the best in the business and once she's decided on an author she will kick down the doors to get him into print. Sure, I've been with her for years and sure there have been no print-ups yet, just rejections, nothing to worry about, what's twenty-five rejections among a thousand possibilities? I mean she is the best I got, the best agent with the best writers and, and anyway I will drop her a line and see what's cooking… Then I will see Louise the concierge and get that over with too, and then I will buy some underwear…

Throw on my shirt and jeans and reset the mousetrap. Who knows maybe there's a second mouse hanging around, I mean maybe when I was seeing one mouse I was actually seeing two or even three, maybe it's like they say when you have seen one you have seen them all.

I head downstairs, unload at the standup toilet on the way, and check out my mailbox. Hunh a letter – speaking of the devil – it's from Robertson! Good news good news? I will go right off and tell Yaku he will be happy, and so will Lydia and so will Celine you can bet. I tear open the envelope.

Nope, no contract in this one, but no rejection letters from Random or Doubleday, just a note from Robertson.

I can tell from the first verb, which is "you are", I can tell from the length of the paragraphs, from the color of the paper, the shape of the words, the odor of the hand which signed it that the news is not good but bad. Robertson wants to terminate our business, says so right here in black and white. Says she is finished with me. "As much as I admire your work, and you know I do, I feel it is impossible to sell these books to a publisher." My work is simply too marginal, she writes, and she hopes that I will be able to sell them on my own, "and I wish you the best of luck, yours truly Eliotte Robertson."

Well fuck a duck.

I try to collect my marbles, what next, what am I doing here, there's no zazen this morning, oh the concierge, ah the hell with all that, the hell with the rent, besides I can't pay it anyway so what's the problem. I tramp back upon the broken steps and along the cracked and leaky walls, enter my twenty-by-twenty-foot room, close the door carefully behind me and stretch out on the bed. Well fuck a duck.

I pick up the letter. What's this thing she says about my being too "marginal"? I pull down the dictionary. Marginal means someone who writes in the margins. So I write in the margins. The margins of what, of life?... Okay let's figure this out, no point kidding myself. By the way they use the word, marginal must mean something somewhere some place on the edge and not in the middling center. Marginal must mean the opposite to what is general, to what is for everyone, like cabbage for instance. Now my writing, if I am to understand its shortcomings correctly, is too specific too personal too intimate too much in the propria persona to be for everyone. I dunno. Does anyone know? Now maybe we should listen a little to our great ancestors the transcendentalists like Emerson and Thoreau, I mean maybe it is a conspiracy like they say – you know a kind of agreement among gentlemen. The publisher arrives for the meeting and the secretary hands him a manuscript which he promptly holds up for all to see. Alright gentlemen, he addresses the boardwalk, how many "yeses" do we have for this here ms, please? Now how many "noes"?...

Anyway, no money is going to be coming from my writing, might as well accept this once and for all... How do other writers do it? probably have jobs on the side. Work for an organization and have salaries and social security and get free meal-tickets at the campus canteen. Sure, most of them are in the teaching business, they are teacher-writers. Or maybe not, maybe most writers just give up writing and become editors or publishers or something.

Ah what the heck! I mean what is wrong with starving anyway? Jarry the great bourgeois-hater writer died this way. Found starved to death in a Paris apartment not much worse than my own. Sure dying is dying but the writer who dies by starvation dies quietly in the serenity of the gods, while the publisher and his cronies die by gluttony, and their bellies explode in a most repulsive manner.

Conspiracy or not, it changes nothing, they got me once again.

This room stinks! Butagaz tobacco smoke and farts, that's it, all my work gone up in fartsmoke. I throw open the window and take in the oxygen from the courtyard, a tiny courtyard its walls sooty-grey and cracked with age cracked from old warring cannonballs and more recent demolition gangs. In fact one of the walls, the one I sleep by, is moving off. They tore down the building next door and this wall of mine has moved off more than an inch into outer space and if you remove the balls of newspaper from the holes in the corner by my head you can see the cemetery right there, waiting below me… Good weather for the crops, too bad there are no crops round here just bodies. (This earth my house the cemetery was once a great battle-field the Eleusinian Fields – or is it Elysium, Elysian? – I should know cause I read it in Plutarch: Once covered in the bodies of dead Gauls and Romans, this soil, soaked in the rains which fell through the winter, yielded in future years quite extraordinary harvests.)

There you go never despair you might still furnish good soil for the cabbage-heads what.

I pass along the wall of bodies in the cemetery and walk over to the department store to change my thoughts to swipe a pair of shorts. Well this department store is a two-storied quadrangle which reminds me of a waste basket made of red plastic, and the people who work here all have soggy heads and it's no wonder they are drowning in this stuff, crush it all together in one lump and it wouldn't bring you a nickel after recycling just alot of poisonous fumes. I mean look at the prices they are asking for this cheap piece of cloth called underwear why it wouldn't amount to more than an amoeba after recycling, a man is a real sucker to pay for this, 30 francs, that's a three-course meal at the Breton. I glance around, wonder if they got the cameras going? Ah the mirrors. Well it looks easy enough. I duck below the mirrors and with my chest almost to the floor I tuck a pair of shorts in my pocket, rise to my feet and walk out fast, the cameras you never know. I return to the room pull on my underwear install myself on the carpet open a bottle of wine roll a cig and just sit thinking: Well I may have lost my agent but I got underwear…

7

> Men like Sagara excused his followers who had committed theft and adultery and trained them gradually. He said: "If it weren't for such persons, we would have no useful men at all."
>
> YAMAMOTO the Samurai

My ears hear the ringing and my eyes pop open and my body is in a standing position in the same instant, 6 am and wide awake. I piss in the sink yawn in the mirror look out the kitchen window looks like it's going to be a just right day today. Makes me feel just like that, just right... Okay so my agent has dumped me, but frankly, I feel relieved. No more writing letters to agents, making photocopies, finding the right-size manila envelopes, sticking on mailing labels, purchasing stamps for printed-matter packages and all that. How does that poem go? O take my hand Walt Whitman afoot and lighthearted...

Ah! Another mouse another one. Dead by guillotine. I drop him in the trashcan in the courtyard and head for the dojo.

The clouds are breaking and the light is coming through kind of chinky and yes the branches of the trees leafless in the cemetery with yet springtime in their bark and yes the birds perched on a frozen wire chirping tee-cha! tee-cha! Am I hearing right are they really chirpin, teacher? I stop in my tracks ears perked and sure enough the birds are chanting the sutras, my ears can hear them.

Lots of empty places in the dojo this morning, just the old hands Lamponéon, Dagoba, Gaitan, Tchang and others not yet mentioned, Bastanks the Viet-refugee, Cavulours the caretaker, Arbalete the one-time terrorist, Ramon the macrobiotic maestro, Raymond the chunky Daruma-cook, Manivel the import-export jock and today's translator; and here comes Valerie the well-bred nurse. Wonder if she transmitted my message. To her father-in-law, the Gaullist minister Whatshisname. He should have received it by now. The message from me to Whatshisname was a kind of apostle's epistle for five grand, something to help me over the hump something for the morale while I compose the up-and-coming Yaku book. I will mention your name, Monsieur le Ministre – why better than that, for five grand I will dedicate the entire book to you! To you and to the master, how is that?

My philosophy of life is simple enough. You make as much noise as you can and then sit back and see what happens. It's like they say, the hinge that squeaks gets the oil. Sure I have written all kinds of letters to all kinds of people, even to Karim – the Aga Khan from my previous life, the childhood one. "It was nice to hear from you MC, after so many years. I was surprised to learn that you have been living in Paris and yet we have lost contact (etc., and): I do wish I could be more helpful in suggesting to you sources for grants but…"

If you want money you might as well go where the money is, you got to be a dope to do otherwise. Nevertheless, asking for things from others is a real pain. Stealing, when you think about it, is much easier, and in a way a much more noble thing to do. And there's nothing castrating about it. On the contrary, without balls you couldn't steal the lollipop from a baby. Without balls there is nothing left but to be a gentleman about it: Please boss give me a raise, please teacher give me knowledge, please Father give me God. Please master give me your transmission. You can designate me as your Dharma-heir, I am ready now.

The sitting begins and right off you can feel it – feel it, not just in yourself but in the others too. Is it the energy? is it the concentration? the concentrated lack of purpose like grasses trees and stones? I dunno… Sensei is saying something about trouble – problems in life – being but phenomena which come like waves, break on the shore and recede, but people like phenomena and so they hold onto phenomena.

The only sounds we hear in the long silence are the patter of pigeons on the skylight. Now Sensei is giving the teaching, he is talking about *zaso* and zaso can mean one of several things (this is how it always is with the Jap lingo, if you're not attentive you might mistake the Buddha for a kitchen sink). So zaso can simply mean zazen or the sitting posture and too it can mean attachment thereof, so Sensei is saying: "If you are zaso (i.e. attached to zaso) you will not attain to the meaning. We must study more from the viewpoint of true zaso, from a viewpoint in which practice and satori are not apart but in unity. True zaso means both to abandon zaso and to be zaso. Now, if during zaso we become completely the zaso itself, completely the Buddha himself, it will be impossible to become attached to zaso…"

My mind wanders… Oh here is something interesting… "I have many strong disciples who have sat with me for many years, but they have fallen, fallen, into darkness," he says "and they stay there in the darkness and I cannot understand this."

I am sitting near Yaku and we are eating the soup mush in silence and he seems sad enough today sitting with his dopes who have fallen into darkness. Maybe he knows he is going to be dead in the equinox and maybe he is thinking damn it, I can't leave my transmission to any of these dopes, I who have worked so hard on them, chiseling sawing hammering nailing sanding and putting them to the great practice, why what will they think in future generations the master carpenter couldn't even make a four-legged table just a rickety old bench and a smorgasbord… I turn my eyes away and suck my knuckles.

All this is too heavy on my heart and I rise up shoot off a quick half-gassho and head for the café, halfway there, hands in my pockets, eyes on the pavement, thinking what it must be like to be a master, what a futile frightful job the world will never know, only a few dopes… But then again is this true? I mean so we are not four-legged tables big deal. Maybe we are all smorgasbords and what's wrong with that? why, didn't Rinzai himself call his first disciple Sansho – the one to whom he gave the shiho – a blind donkey?

Now I am thinking of the teaching this morning, about the great masters experiencing more zazen than any of us, Yaku included. People are people (yes that's it! I snap my fingers) yes and it's impossible for people to be more'n people, more'n perfect people, so what the hell.

I am in the café ordering a beer, looking about. SHE is not about, but there is her new lover some guy not connected with us zasos leaning against the counter looking tough and scowly in his dark lanky body worn-out jacket and grubby corduroys, not a bad looking guy but he's got no ass in his pants, no kidding none at all. Well I turn away leaving him to his toughy scowl, over HER no doubt she's putting his no-ass through the coals for which she is best qualified... Pay your money man and leave.

I move along the rue Raymond-Losserand thinking of love and attachment, of all the good things on earth gone wrong, and I try to understand my own self which is no easy matter especially while you walk, so I enter the dinky café across from the supermarket, go somewhere no one knows me, order another beer and stare down at the counter. I was in love, but no longer you bet. Then I hated her, sure we hated each other that's the truth. And now? Now comes the detachment part. Like now – now she is gone from me, really gone, or almost. I count the days, whew this is the fastest repaired-heart job in history. I feel a sudden surge of love for the master for the teaching, so strong tears come to my eyes. Man I would do gassho to the old bordello down the street, do it right here in the café but for all these gaping people...

Chassepot the kendoman nods to me from the sidewalk, the kendoman is also a plumber and he fixed my sink the other day, Salut! I call out the window. Ah there is Benito the martial arts expert from Milano in town, another smorgasbord come to check out the master. Salut! And salut to you too! says Bastanks half-Viet half-Irish and already half-drunk. Bastanks sticks his head in the doorway and says in chink English: We whip you Yankee asses in Vietnam man! Sure, says I, and how's your uncle pizzaface doing? (Bastanks' uncle is General Ky the Geek you saw in the newspapers, president of South Vietnam and always photoed with his sexy slithery wife – both always in their snappy tight black flightsuits and both in California these days rolling dough in a pizza parlor) and Bastanks with a grin across his attractive headshaved Irish-Asiatic carte-blanche face says, Suck my cock motherfucker!

Ah and there is my old friend Marianne Gottlieb coming out of the supermarché, the poetess looks like a bagwoman – eyes squinty and nearsighted nose large and bumpy hair bleachblond and scraggy clothes in layers in the faded Honolulu colors becoming her and with a voice from the Bronx she says, Well well you've changed cafés I see!... I am happy to see Marianne she is one of my old pals, someone I talk with. I buy her a drink (I always buy the drinks, she hasn't any more money than myself but she knows how to cook up lots of food for a nickel and she feeds me, so I pay the drinks and she supplies the food it's the unspoken entendu). So we get to talking and Marianne says she is happy to see me in another café for a change, not with all those zen creeps for a change, she has met Yakumatsu on occasion and thinks he's the real thing but as for his disciples well she has this quirk about the disciples, finds them frivolous dim wits with big mouths and no manners – not me I am the exception – I mean they are so bloody ugly! the way they wear their shaved-pates like worn-out truck tires you know what I mean. Yes I know what she means; it's not the first time this has been said, she's not the only one in the neighborhood to say it by a long shot, neighbors round here hate our guts, no respect at all for the monks who practice zaso seeking the great way in this world not like in olden times, monks who follow masters are nothing but phony fruitcakes no characters no independent spirit of inquiry, but not me I'm okay... Well Mrs. Gottlieb is no spring chicken she is in her 60's and you can't convince her nohow once she is set on something forget it.

Marianne opens her shredded shopping bag and points inside, Take a look.

– Yeah?

– Well whadya think?

– Lots of food in there that's what I think.

– Yeah but how much, how much you think it costs?...

Marianne rummages through the shredded sack pulling out things: Looka this Camembert from Normandie, milk-butter, calf buttocks, pig bladders, well how much? go ahead and guess.

I scratch my head, I dunno.

– Oh come on.

– Well one hundred francs?

Nope!... She cocks her hip and placing a fist on one of her hipbones and crooking her arm at the elbow in the shape of a handle and herself in the shape of a perfect teapot, she says: Only thirty francs! why I've enough in this sack to stuff you for a week!

Thirty francs, I whistle, thirty francs that's the going price for underwear these days… I tell her about it, I just stole a pair of underwear from that same supermarché, it's the cheapest pair in town and you know what they get for the cheapest shorts in town? Thirty francs! enough to stuff me for a week.

We talk about the price of underwear and I wonder what Peter Pauper wears and Marianne says Are you crazy Peter Pauper don't wear no underwear. Look, she says, you wanna come for lunch?

No, I am on my way to Lee's place, have to see him about this text here and maybe there will be a sandwich or something… I don't go into the matter, don't discuss the text with her, the subject doesn't interest her particularly and besides whenever you discuss your work with the master, people always want to know how much you are getting paid for the job and then you must go into a whole thing about how you work for nothing and the next thing you are trying to convince them that you are not a fruit-cake at all. Sometimes I lie and tell people I get paid – oh how much? Oh enough. But finally when it comes to the nitty-gritty I opt to be a fruitcake over a liar, feels better.

So we talk about the prices of things in general, of the present rip-off index and then we talk about our own work which we can't sell, a real pity, Marianne has rotting wickerbaskets full of poems and stories which no one wants and no one sees, she has been turning them out all her life and she will probably get them published posthumously, sure it will be okay we'll all have a posthumorous laugh but she won't know it. Then we talk about writers and about those who got started in the *New Yorker* magazine…, we are both writers and both New Yorkers but we will never see the light of day through that bi-god bag of constipated phonies, you can bank on that.

Got to get to Lee's eat a little sandwich and do a little business – kill two birds with one stone – and get this sutra business cleared up while we're at it; been walking around with these papers in my pocket for two days now.

Old Lee lives with his lady the handsome Margot in a plush and airy flat between rue de l'Ouest and l'Arbre Sec, that is west of Dry Street, of Dojo Street, and up I fly in the mirrored elevator and along the carpeted floor to the only armored door in the hallway and in I go into a large gay livingroom full of rubber plants daisies tulips mirrors couches stereos and a color TV working without the sound and the talking from nowhere into nowhere and me talking to Lee, Come on Lee you can do it! You can make a book too if you want it's easy. / Hell I can't write my way out of a paper bag. / Look, look, I pull out the papers and hand him the first paragraph which is easy enough and Margot hands me a drink of hard stuff, and I say, See it's easy. Well what do you think?... Lee doesn't answer. Come on Lee you've got the time you're not doing anything.

Sure I know, Lee's so busy with Margot he hasn't a minute to spare. Anyway, this said I glance over at Margot in her leather skirt black stockings black spiked heels striking black hair and sensual rougelipped face, and she winks.

One thing leads to another and we go from peddley talk to talk about Sensei's teaching this morning and somehow we get to talking about Vimalakirti and you know what Dogen says about Vimalakirti? that he was merely a layman; he was one of the Buddha's disciples but he never took the monk ordination and Dogen says that, because of this, old Vim was unable to master many things and he had much to clarify. Well Lee and I are monks, if we are to believe our certificates, and we talk about the not-monks. Did you know that nowhere in the five thousand sutras is there any evidence that the mind of a layman is equal to that of a monk? Now how in blazes can you explain that? I ask, and again: What's a monk anyway? No one knows. Not Dogen, not even the Pope.

I have worn out the ears and then the bottle and now the welcome. Well, I ask struggling up out of the deep leather armchair. Well? Well Lee doesn't answer me again. Well it doesn't matter I drop the uncorrected pages on the marble table anyway, finish off the hard liquor directly from the bottle and take my leave, a salute a handshake a kiss-kiss on Margot's juicy cheeks a gassho at the door and off I go.

Well there were no sandwiches, Lee and Margot weren't expecting me, but there was lots of peanuts and hard liquor and I am on the street again and feeling good again. Ah Paris! Montparnasse! Raymond-Losserand! No place in the world I would rather be than right here on

Losserand. A warm springy afternoon and everything is a-sparkle, the leaves are a-winking and the gutter puddle a-glimmering and the eyes of the Frenchie wenches a-beck-oning. Wow did you see that look she threw me! yeah I pick up speed, first you drink then you cherchez la femme, by jimminy the sight of her knocks the wind right out, I mean that ass those thighs the sway stepping in that door-way like a mare entering the stables... Sure I am one raw sensation. Comes from zazen. Sure there is so much more to control once you have begun the controlling... And just look at that one! And this one here! Holy shit I am going nuts! Alright asshole, I give myself the order, see if you can make it home without drooling all the way, pretend you are wearing a blindfold and a straitjacket, like a theologian caught in a porn show.

I close the door thinking everything will be alright now. But it's not alright. Closing the door is not like think-ing-not-thinking, it's rather like closing the door doesn't really close out anything. I pace up and down, my mind on those hindquarters going through that doorway. If there was only some way... sure I could hang out in front of her door... catch her on the way to the grocery store... Excuse me, but could you tell me where I can buy the *Herald Tribune*?...

I grab my zafu and sit down facing the wall... Thanks to thinking-not-thinking I am very quickly the only living creature on earth in the last place on earth – here where there are no men, let alone women, here where there is nothing, or everything I dunno, and the phenomena slip and slide down my head and off my shoulders like so much perspiration…

The phone rings. Yes? Who's this? / Don't you recognize my voice? purrs a female voice. / Nope I haven't the faintest idea. / I am very disappointed that you don't know my voice, purrs the voice, because you should…

Who can she be let's see it's not her and it's not her and it's not her ah I got it it's her! First time I saw her she was completely in the raw; so was I. It was on the beach, the Playa Formentera, lying in the sand by the water. A knock-out, big tits, long legs, yeah, and I happened by my cock swinging loose and she smiles up at me and her eyes look at my cock and I slip down into the sand beside her, just like that, Miss can you tell me where I can buy the *Herald Tribune* please?...and well the sea-water swooshes in and around our genitals giving a good massage… and yeah I should have taken her right there and then, she was ready for it then, in the given decor, the sun sand and sea and not a peeping-Tom in sight…

And now I get this cute little telephone talk and I realize by the grace of God my chance has come. We set a rendezvous for the following day and I hang up and here we are again, in rut again. God save me the ladies are driving me mad, I am dying for them.

I recall how Frank Harris handled it. Read it in one of his books. What you do is you put your cock and balls in a pot of cold water, preferably with ice-cubes.

So here I am lolling about, my cock and balls in a pot of ice-cubes, listening to the radio, to Bob Dylan singing Times They Are A-changing – yep that's the truth the world has gotten better since he wrote that little ditty, man is freer today and really it's much more fun – and now back to the BBC News, back to places running red with blood, to people being hacked to pieces – yep nothing has changed at all, life is as it always was, a bloody horror.

What's the time? 6 pm time for a stroll in the streets… Walking down Rue de la Gaîté bouncing down the hill of Gaity past all the street action, the moneylenders, dicemen, chicks, spring chicks and old hens, that old whore on the corner looking dirty in her underwear, pass under the neonlit shops and the porno flick featuring Valerie la French in *Fuck Me!* and it all falls off like water on a duck's back, no one, no woman, no idea of one, is going to get me down at least not for long I am like a rubber pumpkin throw it down and it will bounce right back, nothing to do with me at all, it just happens – that's real finesse for you. Oh how indifferent I am to all these haunches and hindquarters as of late. Don't even turn my head, don't give a damn. Now why is this, is it the ice? really is it just *the ice*? Why yes it is. We are like the motors in cars with a cooling system and if you use that system right, if you fill it up with ice-cubes now and then you will have a cool running engine, even on the hills. Zazen may be okay but ice is better.

So I enter the Montparnasse quarter at the bottom of the hill into a kind of bland flatland, really an ugly place, and there's the Dome, Rond-Point, Coupole and here is the Sélect, the last bastion. So I enter the last bastion go up to the bar and right off I hear the news. They have raised the price of beer again. Sonofabitch. So you have gone and

raised the price again, I grumble at Alfred the barman. /
That's right ten-twenty a glass, you want one? / You ought
to be ashamed of yourselves, I tell Alfred right out, your
new owners they're a bunch of chiselers you know that? /
And so's he too! cuts in Painlevy the poorest painter in
Paris can't even pay for a peanut. / Ta gueule toi shut yer
mouth says Alfred. Everybody starts insulting the barman
and the barman says he won't serve that Bougnoul that
Arab at the end of the bar but heck we are in our rights,
with these new chiselers the price goes up five centimes
with every rain there's something creepy and insidious
about their style they are like slowly sucking you dry without your even noticing it, they have slowly sucked you dry
in every café in this city, they have made their money and
their name – les cafés d'artistes à la parisienne – and they
have fleeced you slowly, slowly, and then they have
chased you out, the bum's rush, out of every quarter in
Paris, the Contrescarpe, St. Germain, Odeon, St. Michel, the
rue Cujas, Mouffetard, Buci, and now they are getting you
in your last stronghold, ugly old Montparnasse, already
done it already priced you out of your own places, the
Dome, Coupole, Closerie, Rosebud. It's clear the shop-
keepers can't even allow you one cheap-priced glass of
beer let alone stand you for a drink, fifteen years at the
Sélect and never once a free drink, that's the honest truth.

I count my money, got enough for maybe as many as
four beers. But then I won't have enough for…, I mean a
man must think ahead, like I do, otherwise he is never
going to get there. Okay Barman *donne moi une bière*! I pay

him for the beer but he is not happy, he still has his hand out and his fingers are snapping he wants his tip. It's always the same thing with Alfred, he wants a tip for every beer he serves, for everything in fact! *Écoute mon vieux* – listen old buddy – your tip is included. / No it's not, he lies. / Yes it is! I grab the menu. Look for yourself. / Not at the bar it isn't, says he grinding his forefinger and thumb together like he's counting out banknotes, Show me where it says *service compris* at the bar go ahead. / Hey, I call out to the woman cashier, You hear what Monsieur Alfred is saying? The cashier turns away, doesn't want to know about it, these bums who call themselves *artistes* bah... Well what are you going to do, make a stink over one franc and find yourself back in the street? So I toss the guy a franc and he snatches it up complaining only *one* franc. I turn away in disgust and everyone is snickering, it happens to them too, all the time. And to think the guy is getting rich pinching off the poor no kidding they say he's loaded. And to think that I kind of like old Alfredo, that is I kind of respect him, he is what he is and I mean it's no easy job, no high quality clientele he's got around here, but at least no one goes to sleep on *his* bartop. Taking it from the other angle Alfred is a maestro and even if the Sélect is a rip-off it's the best rip-off in town I am here to tell it.

So I am sitting on a tall stool drinking beer and looking at the dust out the window when in lumbers Don, a man with money. Big Don the American from Hicktown California, beard, sunglasses, crocodile cowboy boots an arm full of girlie mags and a pocket full of shekels and not a stool left in the house. Alfred shoos one of the Bougnoules off a stool, one of those who hang around waiting for a free drink, and gives it to Don and Don nods his thanks to the Bougnoule who slinks off into the shadows, swings up and slaps down his mags on the bar. Don gestures to Alfred just a little jerk of the head and the maestro comes with beers for all of us… The thing is everybody is glad to see Don and not just for his money, he has a kind of warm magnetism hard to resist hard to describe. We get to talking and Don stands me for a couple more rounds and he tells me a bit about his last stint down in the jungle of Africa. He's a foreman or something for a drilling company and he works exclusively with the natives and at night he lies in his hammock and listens to the baboons scream and reads books, even read my own book on zen during this last stint, no kidding, he who usually reads only junk, I am surprised. How'd you like it? / You know being down there with the bushniggers is kind of like being at one of your sesshins you know what I mean? / Sure I know yeah it must be just like that, I nod and order a round this time on me and a couple of twittery girlies pass by on the way to the toilet and now we are talking about girls. He hasn't been laid in a month and he wants to know what the girls are like over at the dojo, and people keep interrupting us and shaking his hand and saying It's good to see you again Don when did you get back? and I say Sure the girls are great and this girl keeps interrupting us with inanities and ineptitudes and Don says over this girl's head, Do they fuck at least and I reply, You know you can find all kinds there it's kind of like a whorehouse you come by and try it out…, and now two girls, no three, are hanging onto his arm talking like dingbats and I yawn and gaze out the window.

Yeah getting tired, been a hard day, maybe I will go take a nap, got to be ready for tonight, got a rendezvous with Caroline.

Mike let's have some dinner, says Don, it's on me.

Food? hadn't thought about that. I should eat something, food is good for you, give you that extra zap, yeah why not…

Don pays the tabs and looks at the girls wondering if he should invite them too for the food, decides against it – dogs all three of them – and heads out the door, me behind. I follow along playing second fiddle, after all he's paying, and anyhow I like it this way being in the shadow it's less taxing. Another thing, you get more from people when you go with them than when they go with you, and so I mold myself to Don adopt his stride, or sort of, a prairie lope (like when me and my brother lived and worked in the uranium prospecting side of things – in homesteads trailers tents first in the Poison Spider then down in Ambrosia over in San Mateo back up in Medicine Bow and outside of Grants ninety or so miles north of the highway – we covered whole counties in both Wyoming and New Mexico) and well it's a pleasure walking with this hick it's not like walking around with a Frenchman from Auvergne or somewhere, even if we are in Montparnasse, in the Gaulic twilight. We lope down the boulevard in silence breathing the air and looking at the lights the reds and yellows and greens. Now we're talking. About the sky. It's a pretty sky, there's a mist in it, lit up faintly by the rays of the sun which

111

has already set off west to Wichita, and it gives a pinkish-ness to the air which impregnates everything and everyone, the bike riders, car drivers, bus riders, street walkers in their shoes and socks and pants and boots and skirts, the func-tionnaires and au-pair girls and now we are in La Mama, pizzeria, and the waitress from Milan is a-slithering and a-sliding serving up the curvy Chianti bottle and the mar-garita pizzas and Don is telling me about his life on a back-woods farm in North Carolina, he moved there to his grandmother's when he was a kid, and I ask him how long he has been around on the continent and he says fifteen years or so, had a house in Tangier for a while, still has it in fact but he rents it out as a private school for European kids… Don was probably into shooting in those days which probably means into dealing and all that, and now he tells me about his job with the drilling company, every few months he is called down to the bush and it's like a cure to him not just a detoxification camp but a kind of thing to con-centrate on. He's a specialist on drill rigging and he's known widely for his talents at retrieving lost piping, even out of the sea he's pulled up broken pipes three miles down in the Atlantic and sometimes, he says, you got these bush-niggers coming at you with their machetes and you gotta be awake. Like in one of your zen sesshins, no dozing on the job right?

Time for my rendezvous in the night. Staggering up the hill full of beer Chianti pizzas lasagnas and tootie-fruities and here's the café La Liberté the brightest and the grubbi-est café on the Edgar-Quinet intersection. Caroline is already here waiting in her furry coat, boots and tight-brown corduroys and looking wide awake. More than me at any rate, goddam tired, there was no zap from that food just the opposite in fact bummed me out completely, went out and focused the remainder of my stamina in the lower belly cranking over all that pizza-mush and I can't get a spark out of my face nohow anymore my face is done in and my mind is amuck. Caroline wants to talk about her up-and-coming courtcase about her kid and her ex-husband but I can't take it, not now, tomorrow, tomorrow. Have another coffee, says she helpfully, have it *bien serré…*, that should do it, get that little zap I am in need of right now, keep my head up off the plastic, goddam it the table is all wet and sticky, yeah keep alert there's lots more action in store for you tonight dope. I caress her hams slip my cold bloodless hand between them hmmmm nice and warm down there, reminds me of a warm bedcover and a featherbed pillow, What time is it ma chérie? shouldn't we be heading home? I wink droopily, time for beddie-bye and the next thing I know she has paid for the coffees and we are walking up the street arm in arm, that's a joke the poor girl is almost carrying me yeah the old samurai and now we are climbing the old stairs and I dunno she is pushing me up by the ass with her head maybe, and I collapse on the bed *hors de combat*.

It is nice and warm in here and I am feeling cozy in the covers and Caroline is sitting on the same covers somewhere heating up the air with lots of hot talk and every once in a while I grunt my agreement, I don't hear a word it doesn't matter another dingbat… Hunh someone is under the covers somewhere sucking me off, oh yes musta fallen asleep. Guess she wants it, oh maaaaaa…

I continue to sleep that is I fake it, see how it goes. Well it goes okay eventually, eventually my mating machine is sticking straight up like a pole in a teepee, in the covers in the sands of the night, head on the pillow eyes closed mouth open in sleep sure, and now you know what she's doing, she's rubbing her cunt against the pole working up a bouguet of salve I guess and now she's straddling the pole but it's too big and she wedges it in with her fingers, yeah just like that without so much as an excuse – me without even a you-don't-mind-do-you, thinks she can do what she will with my manhood whatwith the man out for a nap, and I peek up at her and she's twisting and turning and if my feelings aren't fooling me I'd say she's having the time of her life, no man around to bug her just a cock, and goddam the whole thing really gets me going and the man comes home and he gives it to the lady he rolls her over and gives it to her all six inches and she likes that too even the meat and potatoes you can tell by the way she's jumping about screaming and gurgling, OH OH OH I come aiiiieee aiiiieee aiiiieee stop stop you kikikikill me!!! but I don't stop don't care if I do kill her my hands are holding her big soft ass and big as it is I'm gonna fill it up, with everything and everyone, all the dingbats I saw and heard all day that cow stepping through the doorway, dingbat-purring voices over telephones, swaying thighs every single one of 'em I've ever seen and ever will, I'm goina inflate every dingbat in this dingbat whorehouse yeah the bread's a-bakin' the bed's a-barkin' and I grab her by the hair and force her to look into my eyes burning in my head and say, I'm gonna come you dingbat!

114

8

An ancient once said that a superior man succeeds
his enemy, a mediocre man succeeds his benefactor,
and an inferior man succeeds a man of power.

HAKUIN

The alarm! Holy shit am I wiped out! I am wobbling
about rubbing my face and hitting my shoulders with the
side of my hand like karate chops, or better still, like
kyosaku whacks. In fact, it's Yaku waking me up with the
stick.

I slip on my underwear, scratch my balls and look at
Mrs. Doe-doe, rolled up in the quilt snoring away.
Didn't hear the alarm, doesn't hear the racket, doesn't see
the light. Sure can sleep though. Not a thought in her
head, just a lot of garble. But that's her head, not mine...

Shove my legs into the tubes of my bluejeans stumble
into the kitchen check the trap. Another one. Caught by
the snout, a bit of bacon hanging from the corner of her
mouth. Poor critter's snout almost cut in two. What a
way to die. I do gassho to the poor critter, sorry about
that, but what the heck it was either you or me... I pick
up the trap and hold her dangling at eye level. She's a
fatty alright. Huh maybe she's full of little ones, five little bastards born for nothing but to eat me out of house
and home, and I stare into her eyes, which are wide open
and round and black and staring back at me, right
through my skull.

I sit down on the floor with a cup of coffee and gaze out the window. There's the moon. A pale moon over Paris this morning one mouse will never see.

Out on the street on the Rue Cels and the moon is still there, cloaked in haze and big and round like a dead eyeball; and tall black garbage collectors from the Congo load the truck filling the air with loud clanking noises, in an air fresh and cool, and now I am thinking only of the dojo, man am I happy it's not me who's back there snoring in bed.

We are in the dojo and Gaitan is seated next to me staring blankly at the wall, waiting for the bell. Gaitan lives in a little room down the street no larger than my own and he makes money fixing up people's apartments and overcharging them for the work. He was raised in the street doesn't know his father and his mother is a bus driver and every so often Gaitan waits at the bus stop for his mother to drive by, and then they wave to one another and sometimes if she is ahead of schedule she stops the bus, steps down onto the street and kisses her boy and the passengers never say anything, they are used to it, and anyway as we were saying Gaitan is a wise-ass loud-mouth who does more zazen than me, at any rate…

And the bell has sounded and zaso has begun and you can hear the birds chirping in the yard and the pigeons prancing on the glass roof and the inkin, tinkle! tinkle! and the swishy-swash of kolomos as the master enters, followed by his secretary the slight-bodied French-Italio chick with the high-strung nerves and tiny feet…, and now they too have taken their seats and after some time the master

116

begins to talk about the posture, about it being the highest religious posture in the world, and he goes on, about how the feet are free from the constraints and reflexes of gravity and how the hands are free from touching and grasping and giving and taking and… And you can't hear what he's saying anymore whatwith all the action going on roundabout today all you can hear is the breathing sneezing and sighing and the footfalls of the two kyosakumen and the garbled voice of the master, impossible to decipher, and now the kyosakuman bumps the bell with his stick, the clod, and now what's he doing? the clod is standing on my kolomo and he is pulling me down by the shoulder, or is it my kesa he is standing on? the sacred kesa, my Buddha robe my only one! I fight down an old urge to get up and slug him.

And now it's a coughing contest, everybody is coughing at the same time, but does Yakumatsu mind? he's talking away and no one can hear him and he doesn't care a hoot or he just doesn't notice anything it's the same, and now Lamponéon who is sitting on Gaitan's left begins talking – he is actually talking! – the master is talking and Lamponéon is talking and Gaitan is chuckling and the master is saying, "…this is not the study of philosophy not of theology nor of the way of another, this is the study through body-and-mind the study of the way of Buddha…" Hey that's a good one, says Gaitan to Lamponéon, tell me another, Okay says Lamponéon…, and the two bells interrupt the cacophony, it's kinhin-time and we walk one behind the other exhaling all of us on the forward step of the foot, and there goes the one bell and we all rapidly return to our places back at the wall and there go the three bells and we are all in zaso and Yakumatsu is talking again, this time about Gensha and the dojo falls quiet.

It's about how Gensha killed his father and how he became a great master and transmitted true zaso and saved the lives of countless beings. Gensha and his father are out fishing, that's their job – they are fishermen and they are on the sea off the Chinese coast somewhere it is early morning good and misty and the old man trips and falls into the sea and Gensha extends him the fishing rod and the old man grabs hold and Gensha in a sudden change of heart chucks the rod overboard and the old man drowns. In one flash of lightning Gensha cuts his social ties forever he cuts his karma, no easy thing to do and rows back to shore. The thing is Gensha has this dream this wish to become a saint and now is his chance, he enters the mountains and becomes a disciple to the great Master Seppo. Years go by and Seppo gives Gensha the shiho and Gensha goes off to become an even greater master than the master himself.

Everybody likes the story it's food for thought. Gensha wasn't just any old killer he was worse he was a father-killer. But when you think that Gensha's change of heart happened in a flash of *hishiryo* of *mushotoku* – for at this moment he realized that if his father lived he, Gensha, would all his life remain a fisherman and that his dream to become a saint to become a true monk would once again be dashed against the rocks – one can understand that he just *had* to do it. To become a true master he had to commit patricide no other way around it.

After zaso and after the *Hannya Shingyo* (the Heart Sutra) and after the *Bussho Kapila* (the soup sutra) I get up from the long low table, elbow my way through the crowd, arms flaying about removing kesas all together in five seconds flat, and stand facing the master. Yaku doesn't know that I have slipped the work to Lee and I wish to put him straight, before anyone else does. But he turns his back on me. I drop my eyes, feeling so… so ashamed… so little so common so insignificant.

I walk through the grey drizzle, collar up against the cold, pass the concierge's lodge in the dark hallway, snatch up my phone bill in the mailbox and examine my bicycle against the wall. I dust off the saddle with my sleeve and check the tires, like I used to do when I was a boy. Yeah a nice bike it's a racer, with a Reynolds frame, if you know anything about bikes. I enter the room sit on the edge of the bed and think Okay what's on the agenda today? Let's see there's the concierge and eh there's a dinner date and oh right! that girl on the Playa Formentera, how could I forget her? Let's see rendezvous Sélect 2 pm.

I head over to Montparnasse to the old Sélect. Drizzle drizzle, a good day for a few beers on an afternoon like this. I sit on the terrace by the big windows catch sight of the suckers in the bustle and hustle, the boulot, metro, dodo dingbats, yeah I gloat, a cool beer in hand and the bitch on the beach you haven't quite fucked yet with her dainty little hand in yer dirty old fly while you sip your drink and smoke a cheap cigar…

Well wouldn't you know it the bitch didn't show. Ha and who's the sucker around here? Why she was just stringing me along, lassoed me by the balls, well it serves me right, strange girl calls you up just a voice purring on the phone and what do you do? You drop everything, run about like a rabbit in heat and soak your balls in cold water. Well to hell with her! I leave the table and head for the bar, where I find Jerry.

Jerry is in an expansive mood this afternoon and he stands me for a drink and tells me the latest news. (Now Jerry was once a Cockney boxer and then he became a painter and the last we heard he was pulling in good money with his canvases selling like hotcakes in the London galleries.) But now it seems his art was no longer selling and he had to give it up. Now he is a subway conductor. I was once a London subway conductor, Jerry explains, and now I am a Paris subway conductor… He tells me about driving subways, and then I ask him about his painting, what happened? What happened? says he running his hand over his big face and flattened nose, They just stopped buying that's all. / Yes, I guess that's the problem when you start selling, they can stop buying…

I ask Jerry about himself. He's brooding, got something on his mind. I ask him about it. Well, it seems he just got a letter from his son. From the penitentiary. Over in Liverpool. Tom got caught on a bank job and he's up for eight years.

Anyway I order another round of drinks, on me. But Jerry won't hear of it. Jerry has lots of cash today, he just hit it big on the horses, no kidding he just came from the track…

I push through the swinging doors thinking of Jerry, today his son is behind bars and he makes a pile on the horses.

I cross the boulevard feeling the beer feeling the air feeling the lowering sun, the drizzle has stopped and miracle of miracles the sky is all clear and it's a fine twilight and I am walking up the hill up the Street of Gaity and the light is on my back warming up the molecules and I am feeling fine as a fiddlestick and without a problem in the world.

Oh sure there are always problems little things nothing to write home about, like the rent for instance. I'm only one year behind, this sounds like a problem like a big one but it is not it is nothing at all. At 150 francs a month the yearly rent comes to peanuts and even I can pay peanuts, when the time comes. Sure Karim didn't come through nor did that French minister, but never despair, that's my motto, it's all an illusion – that's another one of my mottoes.

I pass my Reynolds bike in the hallway, I could always sell him, maybe get a thousand. I enter my unpaid place looking around for more to sell, what about the typewriter? that would bring me maybe three hundred, and the quilt? oh about fifty, lemme see there's my alarm clock and there's my stapler and there's... Oh man I must find myself some kind of *source*, everybody else has one, Don got his in the bush, Jerry drives a subway, JP empties garbage cans...

Okay okay. Time to see the concierge confront the issue that is the first step, worry about the next step when it comes... I buy a bottle of table wine from the Arabs across the street and with the note in my pocket and with my hat in hand, as they say, I say Bonsoir Monsieur et Madame les Gardiens and I hand him the bottle. What's the note about Emile, the rent I suppose?

The rent? Emile finds this funny, you haven't worried about the rent for a year, so why worry about it now? No haha, not about the rent, it's about this, and he hands me a card with a Norwegian stamp on it and asks me to translate it for him, it's in English and it has to do with stamps, Emile is a stamp-collector and if Monsieur Emile would send Monsieur Nelsen a batch of French stamps depicting the Eiffel Tower and valued at so-and-so, Monsieur Nelsen also a stamp-collector will send Monsieur Emile a batch of Norwegian fjord stamps valued at so-and-so... Now there you go, it was all in the head, the rent never existed, all an illusion.

Caroline has been invited for dinner at her artist friend's down around Losserand.

The guy is a painter, a young aristocrat and his family has money, gets an allowance from his parents. That's his goldmine... shit, I really blew it. Blew everything! If I had done it right I could be rich today but no, I had to do it wrong – and what did I get? Disinherited.

While the painter and the writer browse through the paintings, C. and the hostess, a sloppily dressed intellectual housefrau who has just had her first baby, prepare the dinner. The two *artistes* talk crap for about ten minutes and then sit down for dinner at the handsome mahogany table with the fine silverware, and what's on the menu Mesdames? What, spaghetti? oh no not again! I lift up a chunk on my fork, hey the spaghetti is all stuck together! I put it back on the plate and reach for the wine. Just then the wife picks up a kitchen knife and starts cutting the spaghetti on my plate. She cuts it into four equal sections, like it was a pie or something…

First I try with a fork, but the pieces have been cut to the size of a pinkie and I can't bend them round the fork nohow. So I do like everybody else and shovel it in with the spoon. Meanwhile the two women do all the talking, yapping the way they do, this time about babies. The lady knows all about babies, she's just made one herself, and it's all very interesting I am sure, I mean Caroline throws herself into the conversation with such enthusiasm, it makes me wonder if she isn't maybe planning on making one herself shortly, on me. I am waiting waiting… for the right moment… and right after coffee I stand up and with a thankyou-kindly-for-the-dinner (even if it was lousy), and push C. towards the door. Thanks again for the great spaghetti, tasted like a pie.

We are in the bed, under the covers and C. is looking at me and knows it's not for tonight, papa is kaput, won't be making any babies tonight, goodnight.

9

A samurai will use a toothpick even though he has not eaten. Inside the skin of a dog, outside the hide of a tiger.

YAMAMOTO the Samurai

Dawn again, daybreak though you wouldn't know it by the light, that is if the light of day has anything to do with the break of day. Day can break as much as it likes, if there's no light, who wants it. I mean I could stay in bed the rest of my life, I could rot away quite happily, five hours sleep last night, why not? I give myself two chops on each shoulder, the wake-up stick, and move, head forward for the sink. My head is hardly under the faucet when my eye catches sight of the trap sitting on the fridge. The bar caught the mouse on top of the head this time, denting it. A real small mouse, must have been the baby and I muse over the symbolic similarities, yesterday the mother and today the baby, it's a message. Everything talks. But I don't always get it as you know.

I unwedge the little tyke's brains from the bar with a screwdriver and drop him out the window – another sacrilege – scoring a bull's-eye right into the open trashcan three stories down. I wave to Jeanine down in the electric-light courtyard and slam the window, whew, lucky the mouse didn't land on Jeanine's head, that would have been a double sacrilege!

Okay, this morning I am going to ride my bike to the dojo. An early morning sprint, that's exactly what I need…,

Hey, where's my bike? The passageway is dark but I can tell right off, something is wrong. I run my hands along the walls, arms outstretched like a blindman looking for his stick, but in vain. My bike has been stolen! My bicycle with the Reynolds frame made in England, gone forever. It's a message from Buddha, it's the cosmos talking to me, or is it just the Reynolds doing the talking – maybe Reynolds didn't like it when I said that I could sell it for a thousand, and so it just took off. Anyway it's all the same, Reynolds, the cosmos – the thing is, you must understand the message. Well I understood the beginning and the rest has got to do with this sonofabitch who dared… I look up and down the Rue Cels ready to choke him to death.

I walk down the dim pavement oblivious of the stars still there, unaware of the clouds on the horizon unaware of the balmy morning breeze unaware of all the changes, without knowing that the whole world is transforming and that I am growing old without knowing it, and the closer I get to the dojo the brighter and the lighter my thoughts become, going from a murky brown to a rosy pink and I think of the guy who stole my bike – who's really not so different from myself I mean I didn't *buy* the bike either – sure I can see him, the kid, he's fourteen fifteen years old flunked out of kindergarten nothing in the way of pocket-money no job and no chance of one, but he likes bikes he knows a Reynolds when he sees one and now he has mine all for free he's riding him right now going for a spin, and I think, why the kid didn't steal it at all. I mean objects change places maybe, but 'stealing' doesn't itself exist – it's just one of those ideas we like to cultivate. Like that's all MINE you know.

And here I am in the dojo, with the sangha, back in the womb wrapped about in the umbilical cord which ties me to those who are here and to those who are elsewhere and now here comes the midwife the master midwife stepping rapidly into the dojo with his secretaries and the inkin-ringer and it's no longer the womb it's the bullring. The master is a toreador and he enters with his music and his archers and prostrates himself in the usual manner and walks along the rows accompanied by the shusso and takes his seat.

The three bells are struck and after a silence the master begins talking, talks about Doctor Bistourix who is else-where, the good Doctor, if not so good a disciple, present in spirit if not in body, present in his letters at any rate. The master has one of them with him now and he reads us part of it, the Doc has been wronged he has been victimized not just by the sangha but by the master too, why he has been hoodooed and hoodwinked and he has had enough… I am amazed. How could old Bistourix ever even think such a thought… Well, Bistourix goes on to explain himself. It would seem, by the letter at any rate, that he, the Doctor, is a master in his own right and equal to Yakumatsu himself! And that if Yakumatsu hasn't given him, the Doctor, the shiho the official transmission it is simply because Yaku-matsu is jealous. Jealous?…

The story is this: Doctor Bistourix runs the Yakumatsu dojo down in Marrakech and so he holds the position of "chef de dojo." Now it must be remembered that it was master Yakumatsu who made a *chef* out of him in the first place – it's all written up in the contract. Anyway, the Doc wanted the shiho and when this wasn't forthcoming, he wanted his autonomy. So he wrote the letter in question, a letter of resignation, he's getting out and taking the Marrakech dojo with him. Sure, the Doc is taking the Marrakech dojo along with him, no kidding, and he's going to carry it on his back to wherever he wanders like a sack full of squirming Lilliputians… Well, Sensei says he will wander and wander and never find the true way, and I shudder and think: ten years sitting with your master and at parting he tells you this…

The master goes on, still in a dejected bitter voice, about those of his disciples who shave their heads in the summer and let their hair grow back in the winter. Such people are just like seasonal vegetables, says he, and once he's finished off the seasonal vegetables he goes on about love and sex. The master is not against love and sex, there's nothing wrong with love and sex, it's simply that women should not go fishing for men and men should not go fishing for women, particularly here in this dojo. "You must not run after nun with shaved head," he says.

Yaku must be talking about HER. Now that she and I are no longer together, she is going around the place exciting all the monks and it has brought out the wolf in them and I tell you the place really stinks if you know what I mean…, and now we rise for the ceremony and she is standing right in front of me, and now we are at the genmai dojo and she is sitting right in front of me and our eyes meet. Well, it doesn't matter because right now I have just discovered a

127

system for disposing of the morning porridge without puking and it's so obvious I am amazed it never occurred to me before. What you do is this, it's very simple, the moment you are served you grab the empty bowl belonging to the guy next in line and pour it in! That's all you do and that's life too. *You pass it on.*

When genmai is over I slip through the sliding doors in the back, don't feel like paying the four francs today, didn't even eat the stuff…

Order a coffee at the counter two thirty without the tip and lean against the Plexiglas door. The metro entrance is directly across the street and the working girls are in their high-heeled shoes and soft cloth and there's one just my type chewing gum and looking dumb and lemme tell you –. I smack myself on the head, Jesus Christ stop it!

Yes well… I look at my watch. Well let's see, could talk with Yaku maybe, if he's still about. Leave a tip on the counter pull up my collar and plow my way through the ladies coming and going like ants in your pants, head back to the genmai room in the courtyard, and there he is, just like when I left him half-an-hour ago, with his first and second secretaries Virginie and Geraldine, and with Lee too, sitting on zafus about the table.

Funny to think how easy it is to find Yaku, he has all the time in the world, he's not going anywhere, no ants in his pants at any rate. Funny too when you think how few people profit by it. Maybe it's because he scares them off. They can't understand what he's talking about. "Practice, practice," they say, "But there are all kinds of practices, sex practice money practice."… Sure, zaso is not for everybody.

Too much knocking about… You know what the kanjis *yaku-matsu* mean? They mean horse medicine (much as the philologists will disprove). So maybe it's only normal he's alone most of the time. Take too much horse shit, I mean horse medicine, and your eardrums might just pop like cherrybombs and your eyeballs fall out like sprung door-hinges.

They are going over some loose pages; Lee, his cowboy hat hooked on the radiator-knob behind him, chewing a toothpick, making corrections, Geraldine telling him what to correct – as if he needs it – Virginie snuffing out a ciga-rette in the butt-filled ashtray. Yaku, glancing up over his reading glasses, announces: "Stanley here is a better writer than Michael Dalley" and Geraldine and Virginie making mimical comments, "Yes he's a much better writer than you are" etc., and looking back in disgust I say, half-vol-ume "What do you tits know about it" – I mean that's how it is, one pleasant word from the boss and the people chirp it in unison; but now that you are on the outs and the boss is giving you the thumbs down treatment, all the people give you the thumbs down treatment.

Grabbing a free zafu, I sit down and say out loud "I am happy everything is working out so well for you" and that puts them back in their places. After all, everyone knows the better it works for them the easier it is on me so what the hell.

I sit quietly doing nothing and they get back into the kusen talking about this and that and it reminds me of myself eight years ago when Yaku had me working on my own first phrases, about the sky being wide and spreading all the way to heaven and the bird which flies realizes the bird itself, to which I re-phrased the last part to read that when the bird flies in the sky it is the bird, which was incorrect, but no matter, I get involved in the work at hand, it's all about words how to get the right word in English to correspond with the right word in Jap which corresponds to the right word in Kanbun or in Sanskrit or rather how to get the true meaning, for this is not the work of words, finally it's not a question of Japanese, Kanbun or Sanskrit (which is just as well seeing that neither Lee nor myself knows anything of these languages) it's a question of feeling the feelings of the master and it all becomes quickly exhausting. So I stretch out in the lazy light, in the middle of the room, on the soup-stained rug, and using a zafu for a pillow and with arms crossed behind my head, I listen to the sound of the master's voice, breathing in the same air and the same cigarette smoke, a mixture of Gauloise, Rothmann and mentholated Kools which once combined make for an incense as fragrant as the Himalayas. Getting into the same mind the same feelings is not just through the brain but through the air and through the molecules too.

Throw away mind and body, says Lee. Throw away? asks Yaku, no, throw *out*. No, says I, slipping on my glasses and leaning up on my elbow, throw *down*… Ah, throw *down*! Yaku looks at me with pleasure, his round ball of a head nodding and saying you understand, you understand. Using my full name, he says, you have had satori.

I take these words without surprise, unperturbed. Not that I was expecting such a remark – though, granted, it is indeed pretty much what I want to hear. These words from

130

the master are not so much official certification (I never quite understood what official certification means), but more as a sign of his affection. Yaku was feeling so miserable in zazen this morning, he was having all those problems with Bistourix and the others, the seasonal vegetables, the wolves and the does, and now he is feeling fine and he likes us and then what the hell this bit about satori doesn't mean more than other things, it's a word, a kind of carrot you dangle in front of a donkey to get him to move, and anyway one thing is for sure: if you take things literally you are up shit creek.

So I have a real dumb expression on my face I guess, everybody is laughing, and I scratch the top of my head, meet his look, eye to eye, and say: True?

True! Michael Dalley has had a good satori. You can teach zen.

Teach zen! With her on my mind? I shake my head in amazement. Yaku is playing with me. He's got me going the feet-over-head-flop. But then again why not? Teach zen, now that would be a wonderful thing to do. Do some good while on earth, and make something of yourself while you're on it... Take my hand Walt Whitman... how does he say it again?

Everyone is laughing, real unadulterated laughter, and the sound of it mingles with the drizzle which is fast turning into raindrops plunking on the dirty skylight like celestial sediment.

The sutra word-work is finished for the day and Lee has broached a subject particularly dear to him at the moment, the subject of money – he wants Sensei to lend him 45 thousand francs. Repayable in two months. Two months, repeats Yaku, his elbows on the low table, his black kolomo sleeves tied back behind his neck, hand holding the kotsu with the fancy string, head without-a-hair looking like an Afghan rug-merchant working out a transaction.

– What interest you give?

– I can give you ten percent, says Lee.

– Americans are very clever at business, muses the master.

– I can put up the collateral if you want.

– What you put up?

– Well, one of my cars. (Lee owns two cars.)

Yaku shakes his head. I want to help you Stanley, but my disciples are always asking me for money so I must refuse them. If I lend you money now and the others find out, then problems problems.

The disciples are asking you for money? I cut in with a touch of indignation in my voice. Well, me I never asked you for a nickel have I? Not only do I never ask you for money but even when you offer me some I don't come for it.

Yaku peers down at me on the rug, but his attention is elsewhere, probably on the deal at hand. But I don't care, I want to make my point, and I continue: You remember the time you told me to come up to your room, that you would give me some money? Well, I never came up, you remember that?

Ah, true?

Sure it's true! Now, how about that, I think. He doesn't even remember. I point to Virginie, She's my witness! Ask Virginie, she will tell you.

Yes it's true Sensei, she nods nicely, Dalley never asked you for the money.

Yaku shrugs, it's all a matter of indifference to him. A master, says he, must never lend money to a disciple, but for you Michael it doesn't matter. I trust you, I have faith in you.

I come to a proper sitting position – it happens that sometimes the body takes over at the least expected moment – and I bring my hands together and do gassho. Thank you.

Yaku turns back to Lee: I want to help you, but first I must consult with Guillaume Tartaban and René Manivel.

When can we conclude it? asks Lee.

Can you sell the cars quickly? Do you have the papers?

Yes I can sell either one right away, says the other knowingly – he knows his cars, one's a Jaguar the other a Daimler, and he knows the market too.

Yaku rubs his thumb and forefinger together and says: How much you get?

For what? The Jaguar is –

No, both both.

For both together? (Lee looks surprised, he wasn't thinking of using *both* cars as collateral.) For both? oh maybe one hundred thousand maybe more.

They must be very good cars, yes?

Sensei is impressed, he has only one car himself, a tin-can he got cheap from a disciple, for 500 francs, and people think he should do better, the great and celebrated Yaku-matsu, not only for decorum but also for efficiency, speed and comfort to his old bones... and suddenly I recall my bicycle: Gone! Gone forever!

Do you know what happened to me this morning Sensei, someone stole my bicycle!... I see myself groping along the walls my eyes round with pained surprise and Yaku laughs and taps me affectionately on the head with his kotsu... You and Lee very different, he observes, Both American but different different.

Sensei rises to his feet and everyone rises with him. He turns to Lee on his way out: You bring me all the papers, and my secretaries will examine them. So I will lend you money.

Lee puts on his hat and we walk out. A fine rain is falling and not having a hat myself, I surrender head and skull to the weather. We shake hands good-bye. Time for lunch, says he. Bon appetito.

I return wet from the rain and look in the fridge. Nothing but a bottle of milk – I can't drink that. Slam the fridge closed, bon appetito pardner... Well old Lee can talk like that, his wet cowboy hat hanging in the shower, Margot serving up the tasteless boiled vegetables – it's for his health his favorite dish – but never mind I have a bottle of wine a corkscrew and a glass, and a typewriter too and a head full of things to write down. So I sit down and hit out the words, not tying them together really, not laying them down in the correct combination necessarily, but just slapping them on the page one after the other in straight lines as if nothing matters anymore.

There is a knock on the door. Damn. WHO'S THERE?!

C'est moi, says a voice a whisper.

I shove the pages under the bed for safe-keeping and say COME IN!... The key is in the door never lock it…

We go through the usual greetings. Bonjour Madame bonjour Monsieur, and Madame informs me that she's on her lunch-break. Her office is just down the street it's her new job at the Tour Montparnasse and, she says, I have only half an hour left and here I am, *me voilà*.

I hang up her coat and return with the wine and a clean glass.

No thanks, I've had one too many already.

Already? It's not yet noon –

We were drinking at work.

Oh?

Champagne, says she smiling casually and with poise. In the director's office.

Oh, I see. I say, come sit here. I pat the bed… What follows is not very novel, can't talk about a work of art, no imagination involved, not even techniques. Just the works of nature. I mean we don't light incense, don't close the curtains, don't hang up the clothes, don't cut the voice on the radio, don't answer the phone, don't pull back the covers, don't prop up the pillows. We just take each other on the spot, belly to belly. No time to lose. Caroline must be back at work and so do I. I gotta write something. Don't know what but something, hurry hurry… But good luck! nothing comes out. Damn it everything already went out the other end…

Man am I hungry! What I wouldn't give for a *hamburger* right now. With a side-order of coleslaw and a pickle. Yes, I had better get back to work, if for nothing but that hamburger. Work for a hamburger and you work for God.

The phone rings and rings and rings.

Hi papa! It's me!

Hiya tootsie, says I taken back. How are you?

She tells me: there is no school tomorrow and she has done all her homework and she wants to know if she can spend the night at my place.

You sure can! Come on over!... Oh and by the way, says I distinctly pronouncing each word, *I have no money today. Get some from mommie for dinner. Okay*?

I hear her pounding up the stairs. She bursts through in her red roller-skates purple cap and chess set, and once she's removed her purple cap green coat and red skates and has a glass of brown milk and gives me a pinkish kiss and an orange candy, I ask her if she remembered dinner money. Yes, she's got sixty francs on her, a fifty and a ten note and she shows them to me oh the colorful French dinner money full of rosy well-fed faces sticking out of castle windows…

10

Among the abbots in all corners of the world today, those who do not know this are too numerous and those who do are too few. The slow walk consists of one breath per step. Take a step without looking at your feet, without bending over or looking up.

NYOJO's words to DOGEN

We are in the dojo sitting one beside the other in front in back knee-to-knee not a cough not a sneeze not a sound not of breathing not even of the heart beating, there is nothing left it's the coffin the communal graveyard.

The bell is struck, mallet against bronze, time for kinhin, zaso in movement… The master passes between the rows looking over his disciples, over their postures, their expressions… and our eyes meet, briefly, impersonally.

There is no need to wink at me! grumbles the master addressing someone somewhere… Wonder who that was… Imagine, someone winking at the master during the slow walk! What a bunch of schoolboys I tell you. Reminds me of the time Bob Peppone and Joseph Baobab pulled waterpistols and started shooting, right then and there, right in the middle of the teaching. One guy, it so happened, got it smack in the nose while he was in the middle of an exhalation and he blew bubbles and went white with apocalypsy – he took the bubbles for Yama, Judge of the Dead, and he never returned… Sure, now I see what Watts was talking about. Alan Watts said that zazen and kinhin are good for nothing but to discipline rowdy schoolboys.

137

The gong is struck and we all head quickly back to our places… We are all seated, legs crossed, backs straight, heads up, hands in the proper *mudra*, exhaling deeply…

Westerners are very pure very delicate at first, says the master. They are very strong-willed very right-willed, but quickly they reach a certain level and go no further…

"…*and go no further*" did he say? I exhale and inhale and exhale and inhale…, I mean where are we supposed *to go* anyway? Yaku, aren't you always telling us zazen is good for nothing?

Good for nothing. We stretch our backbones, breathe in-and-out deeply and easily, with mind on nothing much – like so many rowdy schoolboys – and once again everything kind of vanishes, it's all so very unimportant, like when you pull anchor and set sail it's always for the horizon nothing else matters, just catch the wind and head out…

Yaku is talking about the three minds and the three worlds. It's from the *Shobogenzo*. "This is very complicated, says the master, Very intellectual. I have been studying it for two days now and my head hurts. Too much thinking, tired tired… If I die it is because of the *Shobogenzo*…" This is what he says. He says the *Shobo* is killing him!

Silence again, nothing, not a sound, and it goes on and on. Then: click! click! Coming from overhead, the skylight, feathered bipeds, pigeons. The skinny winter pigeons starving in the zero temperatures of the three worlds, with no one to feed them, except maybe some old ladies…

"One of the disciples has just died, Yaku announces, Madame Mertzel."

The news hits me like a kyosaku between the eyes. Mertzel was very old, but this didn't seem to matter, she was here just last Sunday...

"I went to her apartment, she was very pretty before she died, says the master, I am very moved by her death."

11

He who would progress in the Work must learn to earn his living with his left foot.

GURDJIEFF

You wake up to the new day.

And when does this day start, you wonder? Why the moment you awake of course. The moment the day starts, you wake up yes. And night? Night is the other side of day, it's when light is dark. Or when the ghost is in the cave of Black Mountain as one master once said.

I open the window stick out my head and look around. Nondescript little houses crumble in the rainy darkness, streets no wider than evacuation trenches regurgitate in the distance. Another bad day.

Flick on the light in the kitchen and examine my face in the mirror. Any razor blades left? No none left. Too bad, guess I won't shave today. Didn't shave yesterday either so why bother about it today.

Pull on my pants, same old pair with the same old shape at the knee, already knee-deep in yesterday and I'm only just starting…

…And here we are, thirty minutes later and knee-deep in the dojo, listening to the master. He is talking in English and the translator is translating him into French but something is wrong with the translator today, his name is René Manivel and his girlfriend just dumped him for someone better and his voice is all messed up, he squeaks and stutters and can't get it right and those who only understand French aren't getting it right either, but the master doesn't seem to care – come to think of it the master has never worried himself over getting his point across, through words or otherwise, he talks and teaches and doesn't care a rap if we understand or not.

The soup is finished and the place is emptying out. The hairless master takes out a Rothmann, the hairy Viviane snaps out a match and all the smokers present follow suit, the blackhaired secretary Virginie pulls out a Gauloise, the silverhaired Stanley pulls out a mentholated Kool and me, the lighthaired Mike, I don't pull out anything and Stanley, who has the ability not only to see right into my pockets but also to read my mind, throws me a Kool and we all drag it in and out and in again, like a bunch of Indians, and then we get to talking, what's-new-in-the-sangha kind of thing, like what the dickens is wrong with the translator, René Manivel? Well, it seems René Manivel's lady-friend has been going at it with the tenzo, the cook, seems she's been going at it for a while now, and RM never noticed a thing, too busy translating, but that's life, blind yourself with the holy, and by god the profane will get you right in the bullet hole: sure, while monsieur translates for the master, madame screws up a storm in the dish cupboard.

Me and the ladies, Virginie, Viviane, Geraldine, Emma and Natasha smile slyly over the poor guy's bad luck, sort of like my own but never mind, the master isn't of the same mind, he doesn't like it much when his disciples have couple-type encounters. but what can you do, excommunicate them, beat them with the kyosaku?

Someone starts counting up all the disciples for whom the master has conducted marriage ceremonies, and who are no longer together, about a baker's dozen. That's it, Yaku announces, I won't marry anybody anymore!....

I recall the last marriage ceremony he performed, for Baobab and Ida. Earlier during the kusen, the master had said, "Baobab and mademoiselle asked me to marry them; even during the sesshin they think of making love, so surely with this ceremony their bad karma will finish..." and then during the actual ceremony he said, "It is not necessary to go with other people, now you must concentrate on mademoiselle..." Yaku and the newlyweds interlinked arms and drank wine out of the same glass. "I hope your marriage," said the master, "is a great success..."

Well today Baobab and Ida make up the Baker's dozen of broken couples but Yaku is not angry just sad, "This is the great crisis of the West."

We sit in silence while Yaku reads through his mail. Then we start talking again, about this couple thing. About me and HER, about me and the Queen of Sheeba. The story is almost public property, it happened not so long ago and everybody saw it go, saw it take off, couldn't avoid it, I mean our love rose up lovely like a heavenly arch... and came down quick like a brick shithouse for two and now that the show is over curtain and all, Virginie wants to know if I am with someone else.

Yes I guess you could say so.

Who is she?

You know, the one with me at the café yesterday.

The brunette with the frisée hairdo and the fur coat? What does she do?

Oh nothing much, I shrug can't remember.

Has she money?

No. The fur coat belongs to her mother and –

From where then do you get your money Mike? cuts in Emma Schweitzer.

Well from nowhere I guess.

How do you pay your rent?

I don't know. I mean I don't. I mean I'm about a year behind.

And how do you pay for your food?

Food? Why I get my food in the local garbage can.

The Restaurant Breton. It's so bad they give it away.

Don't play the fool Mike, observes Emma, You get your croute pain, your bread-money, from your little girlfriend, everyone knows that.

Bah! I spit... Nothing galls me more than to be taken for a gigolo or worse a parasite.

Then from where? someone persists, From your writing?

Are you still writing? asks another.

Yeah.

What do you write about?

Oh about myself I guess.

Just about you?

No not exactly, I write about you too. About you and about you and about you and about all this stuff, I gesture with my head to the people, the walls, tables and chairs.

That sounds *very* interesting, says the secretary and she really means it too – she thinks a book about us printed in the United Stars of Amerlok is just about what's needed now – and she continues her inquiry: Do you send it out Mike? Does anyone ever read it?

Well, héhé, I laugh stupidly, the editors do. That's my public. It stops there.

Ah yes? And the book you are now writing? Do they read that one too?

You mean *this* book here? The one about us? Yes, they have read it.

And what do they think of it?

Almost every editor in the business has read this book, says I. Any editor who knows *anything* about zen has read this book, says I again, with a smile.

What's it called? cuts in Geraldine, What's the title?

It's called *Horse Medicine*!

And what do the editors think about *Horse Medicine*? continues the secretary.

I don't tell the gathering of their disapproval of the book's slipshod thoughts and loose words – no point bringing everyone down – and so I just say: I don't know really. What do they think, do they think? good question, I dunno.

And when you went to America last month, asks the red-haired Viviane who writes books herself and is always open to a tip or something, Who did you show it to?

Oh forget that, I reply annoyed. Bantam Books, shit!

Oh man, I won't be quick to forget that trip: went back to New York City with two manuscripts, and, well, Mrs.

Banters, Editor-in-Chief in the Eastern Spiritual Department, was quite put out. Banters didn't much care for the way I mixed religion and sex and, really, she didn't like my style at all. Mr. Dalley, she summed it up, you simply *can't* write!

Well can you beat that? And then I recall this other guy from Dutton, and the one from Grove and…

So we are sitting on the floor and I don't tell them any of this of course, and suddenly Yaku says: How many years you write? Ten years twenty years? And never published?

Yaku has asked me this before and this time I don't know what to say – Yes or no? – Whatever I say it sounds too silly, so I say nothing much, and he looks at me with a big clear grin and pats me on the back:

I understand your karma, says he, putting out his filter-tipped cigarette, Mine was not so different when I was your age, but then it changed.

Well I hope mine changes, I reply, and soon.

It will change. When you are in your fifties. Your karma will change and you will have what you want and you will be a big success.

Really?... (I count on my fingers, why that's almost fifteen years off). Sensei, I question him, will success come to me in the early or in the late fifties?

He says nothing.

Will it come to me through my writing?

No.

No? Not from my writing? (I am speechless, then after a moment): Well, from an inheritance then?

No.

Then from where?

Yaku looks at me with amusement (or is it bewilderment?) picks his kotsu off the table (the little round-topped staff) and points with it to the floor.

I look down. All I see is the rug. I imagine the floorboards under the rug and the ground under that, the earth, with its muck and with its rock and its minerals. I think of ore, the Lotus Flower in the mud, ore in the muck. And at the same time I think of my brother Peter over in New Mexico and I wonder if we are still holding the rights on those uranium claims we staked… up by Grants…

I come out of my reverie and ask the master another question, but he is elsewhere, talking to others, about other things…

So Yaku says I'm going to be a big success, sure I always knew it, my rich background and all that, sure I'll be back where I started, a pocket full of cherries picking up the ladies and buying drinks all round at the Sélect.

I think of Yaku, of our *mondo* together, along with the kotsu, 'it will come from the earth'… Now what else could come from the earth besides uranium? Let's see there's rock and dirt and trees and plants and flowers and – ah yes: pot, marijuana, hashish! That too comes from the earth. Know all about that. Good business too… if you don't get busted… like I did.

Looking at the master. His skin is turning color, seems he's got the yellow sickness (everyone is talking about the master's pancreas these days which is causing him the strange color) but never mind, he's his usual self, color notwithstanding, eyes bright in their yellow sockets and face awake with softness… My glance drops to the clean white collar of his kimono, the black cotton robe, the rectangular brown rakusu, and I recall the time, not so long ago, when he lived in a basement and slept on burlap… and I think of the Bodhisattva treading in the muddy muck… and now suddenly from somewhere just behind the brain I understand, he points to the earth, sure success from the earth means success on the earth, in the here-and-now.

Some moments elapse. I rise to my feet, face the master, place my hands together palm to palm and bow. I would have preferred to do *sanpai* to him, but you know how it is, whatwith all these people and all. I mean I do gassho almost every morning, but anyway today I mean it more than before…

Heading home, not a long distance, not a short one, pass by the bakery, the flowershop, the plumbers, and at the end of the block the squatters' stronghold. Two squatters squatting on the front stoop, faces jagged, stony, smoking a joint, smoking a flower, their first today.

Climb the wooden stairs, open the wooden door, recently reinforced, enter the room lit by a ray of tame winter light, light the stove, unhook the pot from the wall, throw in yesterday's spaghetti, a hunk of margarine, salt and lots of pepper… Lunch finished I turn the radio dial to FIP, and from my hard bed of success, I dig the sugary music.

12

The mouth of a monk is like an oven. Just as an oven burns both sandalwood and cow dung without distinction, our mouths should be the same.

KATYAYANA SONJA

Ringa-dinga-ling! I pop up like a jack-in-the-box flick on the light and look about. The quilt slips off my shoulders ooooh! it's cold in here, cold as an igloo ooooh can't make it today *tant pis*. I grope for the quilt and snuggle back under.

Certainly, zazen practiced regularly and on a daily basis is very important. We all know that. But every day of your life? No, can't make it this morning…

And besides who cares anyway? It's not the chain-gang, not like going to the office, no one ever says "Hey, where's Mike this morning?" Not here, tantpis, no one cares…

I snuggle under the cozy quilt – a gift from Caroline – snuggle up among the cozy cushions wrap myself about my cozy little girlfriend, sure too cozy to go to zazen, cozy good for nothing morning…

Caroline is up bustling about getting ready for her new job. Now it's her turn, can't lay around like me… "And where is little Miss Caroline this morning?" says her boss. "Not here! Why she is fired!"

How's the job, I ask her. Selling any books lately? Sure, she's made a few sales. Nothing like her boss though. C. tells me about her boss again – he's the same one who

served her champagne in his private office the other day –
and it seems he can sell them so fast you would think he
was an enchilada vendor and not an encyclopedia man at
all.

"Take care of yourself," she calls from the door and
blows me a slow kiss, "And don't forget your luncheon
rendezvous."

"Yes… and you too," I call back, "Have a happy…
enchilada…"

I shave with a new blade from C., pull on a pair of
shorts, so old can't recall who gave them to me (maybe I
bought them myself, who knows back in those days), a pair
of flannels from Bernie a clean shirt from Chevalier –.

Chevalier, he is the gentleman who gives me money in
return for my writing. All he wants are the pages. He can't
read them because he doesn't read English, but that's just
as well, he has faith in me anyhow, he doesn't care about
style or even content no, Chevalier doesn't care about anything like that, all he cares about is the *proof*. Does Mike
write or not? All Chevalier does is count the pages and the
more the better, money-wise at any rate.

And what's in it for him, you might ask? Why,
nothing not one single thing. Mushotoku, no profit.

Anyway, my rendezvous is with Chevalier and it's
right now, at La Coupole.

THE LANDING: What a stench! Kind of like urine, dogshit
and human rot all rolled into one. Must be Jeanine and
Milou her dog. Poor wretches… What's that? an empty
bowl on her doormat. Maybe she's doing a begging num-

ber, while she sleeps kind of thing. Well, if she thinks I'm going to drop a franc in that bowl she's got another thought coming.

THE HALLWAY: A letter in the box. Well well, a letter from HER mailed to me a month ago, via New York and other places… I read it through and through, like hearing a dialog of another time another world… I was perfectly content one minute ago, and then comes this letter out of the blue and bingo! My heart aches my head hurts and the world goes by without me… But not for long by god: there's this method which I practice pretty regularly, has to do with the position of the backbone, stretch it near the bottom, at the fifth vertebrae to be precise, eyes before you, mind your feet, the true samurai.

THE STREET: Rue de la Gaîté, panhandlers, pornoshops and patisseries. Lots of dainty little pastries, pies and puddings… Time for lunch, step up the pace, at the bottom of the hill is Montparnasse, the Sélect, the Coupole…

THE RESTAURANT: The maitre d', a friendly old chap in black, leads us past the bouquet of flowers in the middle, a gay collection of roses tulips and whathaveyou weighing half-a-ton, and shows us to a table. Nice enough place, nice light – nice old daylight for a change – nice old waiters legging about on their last stretch, nice old clientele too, people laughing, jolly faces, jolly jokes, nice to see everyone stuffing themselves, and then over here we have the ladies in fox collars nibbling away on salad roots and grasshoppers…

Talking about ladies, I'm kind of like a lady myself in this deal (Chevalier is wearing the pants today) only I don't wear a fox collar and don't nibble grasshoppers, me I eat a fat rolled up fish called a roll-mop, a piece of meat the size of an encyclopedia, a crepe the size of an enchilada, potatoes the size of softballs, Burgundy wine, ice-cream in its licorice, and half a dozen cognacs for the road.

The meal over, Chevalier counts the pages and hands me a note. 500 francs. Now there's a Bodhisattva for you, paying out of pocket 500 francs for what no one else would pay a cent.

Walking up the hill, the sky is okay and so am I a piece of meat under the belt and a roll in the pocket, past the patisseries and the pornoshops and…, ah yes, we are now approaching my favorite pornoshop, it's called *Porno Hard* and they stock my favorite photo album, "Les Nichons de Marion" (The Tits of Marion), and am right now wondering maybe I should go inside, I got the money got the time got the… Hehe, I know all about it, go into *Porno Hard* and in five minutes you are back on your bed beating your meat like a goonydick, no not today thankyou.

What should we do now? spend what's left or save it for tomorrow? No, better yet I'll *invest* it. Invest it with the concierge, something toward the rent, before there's none left… I buy a bouquet of daisies at the Ga té rip-off flowershop and visit monsieur et madame les concierges.

Louise is cleaning the dishes and Emile is picking his teeth and watching TV… Have a good lunch? Me too, very good, thankyou. I sit down on a plastic chair and Emile pours me a brandy, my seventh so far. We toast to one another and to the tenants, all decrepit but never mind, I also give a big toast to Barjoc, the owner of the building…

We toast, Emile grumbles, drinks his brandy and says: Barjoc, he's a veritable crackpot, you don't know that?... No, I don't know. I have met Barjoc on occasion and he seems a normal amiable sort. But more important than that, Barjoc never bugs anybody for the rent, why I haven't paid it in over a year and Jeanine my neighbor hasn't paid since her husband died more than a decade ago, and this is certainly worth a toast don't you think?

But Emile isn't of the same mind. Barjoc never brings the quittances, the rent receipts! He doesn't give a bloody damn! Saves on income taxes and to hell with everyone else!

Now, what's wrong with that? No one pays and good riddance.

You think so? says Emile... He looks at me like I don't know anything... Look at la mère Michele the cripple on the first floor, at old Perier the drunk on the second, at le Taré, at the retired undertaker what's-his-name, they have all gone and lost their social security... Emile gives me a refill... Without their quittances, without proof, you can forget it. Forget it all! Retirement pensions! life insurance policies! room & board allowances! disability pensions! unemployment benefits! paid vacations! reduced travel rates! redemption benefits! bonuses! discounts! refunds! rebates! reduced rates! compensations! personal savings! premiums! – Emile stops his tirade only once he's out of breath and red in the face – merde ou quoi, shit or what?!

Without the "quittances," explains Louise, who's going to use his own savings to fix the holes in the steps? the broken plumbing? the leaks in the roof? you know Madame

Douche? her room is on the top floor… she has to use her umbrella to walk across the room – yes exactly! Why, her rug is just like a sponge… whatwith all the rain we've been having lately.

I see their point. Hadn't looked at it that way. Don't have the security myself, didn't know security could cook your goose so bad. Well live and learn.

We turn to the TV. A program about insecurity in the streets. What people will do to one another for money is just awful, no question about that, and Emile, who's in good shape starts talking politics, left, right and center. He lays into the Bougnoules who are all dope dealers and then he's onto the local tax collector and even the news commentator himself: les pauvres enculés, poor assholes! Do we deserve this, oui ou merde?!

The ads come on, a sexy nude gazelle with flowing blond hair down to her rectum rubbing herself with a bar of bright pink soap. Sure, advertisements are a good thing, saves people from going berserk and shooting one another…

By the way how's Jeanine doing these days?…

Well it seems her plumbing clogged last Christmas and she hasn't cleaned since. That's more than a year ago. It seems the lady keeps throwing toilet paper and dogbones down the sink and Emile, who until then always fixed her pipes for her, won't touch them anymore. It's like climbing into a garbage can going in there. Gets worse and worse! He shouts. Last time I got sick, vomited, I'm not lying to you, isn't that so Louise?

Not only doesn't Jeanine have running water, she does-n't have any electricity, doesn't have a flashlight, not even a candle to go by, let alone a pack of matches; she doesn't have any heat either, Louise gives her clothes on occasion, saves her from freezing to death, I guess, but is she eating at least?

Eating? Eating what? says Emile.

Sometimes I give her our leftovers, says Louise.

Huh! Almost every day you mean, says the husband, And not just leftovers either. What did you give her yes-terday, Louise?

Last night I left her a bowl of cabbage soup.

Oh, I cut in, is that *your* bowl in front of her door?

Yes, nods the lady, I leave the bowl on the floor, knock on her door and run off before she opens up, the smell you know.

And what about the dog? I ask.

To hell with the dog, grunts Emile blowing his nose on a scrap of rag, We can't feed the dog too!

No, of course not. What I mean is maybe she can eat the dog.

Eat the dog! That's a good one. My God you see that mongrel? merde I would rather starve to death!

That mongrel as you call it, says the kind-hearted wife, happens to be her only companion in the entire world.

Sure, no one else can go near her.

And what about her daughter? I ask.

The daughter doesn't want to know her. They haven't seen one another for over 25 years. A matter of social standing.

Another ad flicks over the screen. The BNP bank, another pretty girl depositing a wad of bills or something…

Time to go. I get up, reach into my pocket and give Louise 200 francs towards the rent. She's the book-keeper and she writes it down in the ledger. We say goodbye and I head up the steps.

Thinking of Jeanine, bad luck for one is bad luck for another. I curse my luck. Of all the people to have next door. The worst kind of people to have as neighbors are people worse off than yourself. I mean now that I have some ready money myself, and she hasn't a sink to piss in anymore, it just doesn't seem right. Maybe I should give her some loose change or a little note or something. I mean it's not me starving to death it's her. Let's see, I've got two fifty franc notes in this roll, could give her one of them, what the heck… I hesitate at her door. Giving her the note is a little risky. The stench I mean, and what if she decides to embrace me, ugh… I will do it like Louise, drop the note on her dirty doormat, in full view, bang on the door Jeanine! Jeanine! and enter my own room, facing hers about six feet off, and quickly close the door… I wait ears perked, and wait and wait. Maybe she didn't hear me. I dash out, bang again, JEANINE! JEANINE! and dash back. Still nothing. Maybe she's dead already… I'm about to take back my money – no need to pay the undertaker too – when I hear her working at the lock, the locks (no kidding!) on her door. Finally, the door opens. She's picking up the bill I can hear her. Now what? no sound at all. I remove the key and peek through the keyhole. Gahhh! the smell, gotta hold my nose at the same time, can you believe it. Well, there she is, in a tattered coat and scarf, her usual winter housewear, holding the bill up to the light of the window (she broke her glasses last year and has been blind ever since). Milou! she calls, Milou! Viens vite my little cabbage head!... And out of the dark hole comes little cabbage head, wagging his scrawny tail and jumping about, like he knows it too, there is a dogbone in the air he can smell it already... And when they return a little later, it's with the provisions, a plastic bag full of vegetables, a stick of bread a bottle of milk and I don't know what else. Oh the happy lady! Oh the happy dog! Now that was worth witnessing, Mike.

Night has fallen, 9 pm, Caroline and I are at the Restaurant Breton on Losserand waiting for dinner. Yep, today is eat-day, everybody eats today, Chevalier, Jeanine, the dog, C. and me... Anyway, dinner for two and it's on me, I'm paying tonight, big treat. Of course, the Breton can't compare with La Coupole, in fact sometimes the place can get downright grubby. This is not to mention the decor, always the same, same old sea things right out of some two-bit Melville, a moldy mollusk shell, a rusty harpoon, a broken tiller, a rotten rope, but it's the fishtails lying on the tables and the trampled food which really get you down – this and the meal itself. Well, no need to go into detail but on this particular evening they serve up a couple of plates of hagfish, mucous glands and other refuse...

The Restaurant Breton used to have a certain class, cheap clean and okay food. But now God knows what's happening. Things keep changing, can't count on anything, not even food finally.

I call for the waitress. 55 francs tip included, give her the money, plus a couple francs extra, and count up what's left... Not much, enough for tomorrow if we stretch it out... Good idea, be responsible for a change, get yourself a ledger and a new ballpoint pen and do a little bookkeeping. Get back to your spaghetti, genmai, coffee and a bottle of wine. After all, one meal a day can take you a long way, tomorrow and tomorrow...

13

7 am. Dark and raining. I break into a run, shoes are leaking, glue giving way I guess, and while I run I see – in my mind's eye – Vercingetorix and his people running over this same ground, over this same rock and muck, under these same pissing skies, and I am running with them, after all we are not so very different, same skin and bones, same wet hair and beards.

The vestibule: Nod here and there to the people, remove shoes socks jacket and pants and replace them with the black robe, the same one monks wear since God knows when, same cloth, same color, same cut (nothing much changes in this place), and I rub my hair dry on the large sleeve of my robe and head for the dojo across the yard. Splashing barefoot through the puddles, one running in front of the other, leaving our robes wet to the calves. I bang my feet on the tatami, almost numb with cold, nod to a few more people and sit down... There goes the bell, the starting bell, like the gun going off in a gold rush, and I bow and begin.

Nothing but the sound of rain on the skylight, washing the void above, door to the skies, way to the gods, eye of Buddha in the air rushing through the thorax, filling the lungs, then out again, out through the pores in the skin, out through the tips of the fingers and the toes.

A long silence a deep pain, legs knees and back, nothing to write home about – and the master starts in:

"Mountains rivers sun moon stars the big land, mind-land, treasure land and the heatless pond (i.e. nirvana) are actualization of mind," says the master. "All these lands are based on the experience of satori and are therefore manifestations of *shiki soku ze shiki*. Mountains rivers etcetera are seen differently by heaven people and by earth people, when you attain satori the viewpoint of mind becomes universal and all existences become one mind…"

"Is this one-mind coming or leaving? Is it inner-mind actualizing itself or –"

The master suddenly cuts himself short to bawl out the translator. It's René Manivel again and Yaku says he's messing it all up. "René (he pronounces it Lené as the Japanese are wont to do) Lené is no longer my translator! From now on Lucien Dagoba will translate!"

So Lené is getting the boot. Well, it's about time. Sure, everyone feels sorry for the poor bugger, it's a real punch in the nose, we all know that, but Dagoba is better and let's get on with the show man:

"Is it outer phenomena actualized from our inner mind or is the actualization of our inner mind coming from the outside? And when we are born is another mind added, and when we die does this mind escape?…

"All the cosmos is one-mind. All existences are the actualization of self-mind. So how should we think when we study mind? Usually we think of natural phenomena: Mountains rivers sun moon etcetera as outside our mind. But these are mind itself.

"Do not deduce from this that everything is only inside your mind. Abandon notions of outside or inside, coming or going. Undivided mind is not outside or inside. It comes and goes freely without attachment. Every thought is inde-

159

pendent, newly created, vital and instantaneous. So please," the master enjoins us, "repeat this method of thinking, and form it, build it into your daily life with only the one mind of the Three Worlds."

We are now in the genmai dojo and I have finished my soup and am looking at the master who isn't looking at anybody really, his gaze being neither far-off nor close-by, his mind invisible, and his form too – or almost – so frail so peaceful, actually. I think of his wonderful words this morning, and he meets my gaze and we both smile with the eyes and I know full well he can see me to my marrow, his face bright like a mirror reflecting my own, without judgment…, enchantment maybe.

14

According to the scientific philosopher Wittgenstein, something went wrong with the physiological development of the human brain sometime around the Pleistocene Age.

I walk through the snowflakes. What a mystery! I mean from a sad sky of dirty garbage fall these white-winged beauties of paradise, now isn't this something!

Back at the dojo the monks, bodhisattvas, dakinis and other devilish dumbbells sit on their zafus waiting for... why, waiting for the bell... Margot the leg-lady, Greta of the big tits, Smartie the smart-aleck editor, Tamponard the Sore-bun-boy (I mean Sorbonne boy), Dagoba and Manivel the two translators, Stanislas the paregoric hophead, Tartaban the Swiss musician, and Bocalo the rightly well-paid philosophy professor. (Did you know that Heraclitus was born on the same day as Buddha, that Socrates wore an exact replica of the Buddhist kesa and that Pythagoras expounded on the theory of interdependence, transmigration and reincarnation? Bocalo the professor told me so.) Anyway, Bocalo is sitting quietly, facing the wall, legs crossed, head erect and without the slightest movement; he's not looking at the door, like I am, to see who's coming this morning, he's not looking at the girls, not looking at Margot and Greta and... and why, Bocalo is not looking at anything, is not looking for anything, Bocalo is a good example to all of us.

So the monks and company prepare themselves for the holy work ahead, purifying the outside by cleaning up; clean the throat with coughing, the nose with sneezing, pick the teeth with a matchstick, twig or fingernail, then brush them with the tongue, and vice versa, brush the tongue with their teeth, rub the sleep from their faces, pick the gum from their eyes, use the clean sleeves of their robes for a towel and rub it over their heads, wipe away the dirty snowflake tracks, push the hair back off their forehead, blow the dust off their spectacles, massage the neck, back, legs, knees, ankles, adjust the cushion, lift their balls up over the fleshy insides of the thighs, ventilate their intestines with a good fart, straighten out the white collar marked off by the black kolomo, adjust the kesa over the left shoulder…

Bong! Bong! Bong! the copper bell is struck. Everyone stops what he is doing, does gassho and takes up the posture, everyone except Bocalo. The master is approaching the dojo, you can hear the tinkle of the inkin growing louder… crossing the yard… entering the door… It's no big deal, he enters the dojo in this fashion, behind the chiming of the little bell and in the company of his secretary, every morning year in year out, but Bocalo (our good example) twists his neck round like a monkey… The master walks to the altar, then he sits down…

And now, in the deep silence, his voice purifies our insides:

"Undivided mind is not concerned with big or small, far or near, being or non-being, gain or loss, satori or non-satori, life or death. Undivided mind is beyond opposites… The way is to attain stable undivided action beyond the world of relativity."

Dagoba is translating today, bouncing along with the master taking in the English and spinning it off in French, thinking of nothing, knowing nothing (he doesn't even know English, no kidding) but does this matter? No, he would understand Yaku even if he spoke in Swahili, it's like music, like a dance, rhyme and rhythm, tune and tone, it's *I shin den shin*, from mind to mind, but whatever, I am no longer listening. I am listening to myself instead, not because it's more interesting, far from it, but because that's what happens however you do it, just mental aberration, goes way back, back when we began thinking in the first place, during the Stone Age…

To cut the inside phonograph I follow my breathing, lower abdomen fills out, the diaphragm is sinking sinking, and the air pours into my lungs, then a contraction – must be the abdominal muscles – and now the breath is being pushed up and everything is rising flowing upward, on its own, calmly, steadily through the upper lungs, the thorax and out the nose. So my body is in complete control of the mind, no more yapping in the brain, the brain is clear and wide awake. This is what it's about, one-pointed concentration, *shikantaza samadhi zanmai o zanmai*, and this is what I live for, for zazen, with the master…

"A new mind is not created when we are born," says he, "mind is not coming from anywhere. Mind is only visible realization of cosmic-mind as self-mind… When we die we do not decrease or finish our mind and it does not go anywhere. It only becomes invisible… It is only the arising and vanishing of the one cosmic-mind, all our body-mind is *ku*, originally no increase decrease or death…"

(Yes, just as I said, the madness of man goes on and on, from the cavemen onwards, from the first to the last, like karma like transmigration. Maybe this is why Sensei says a master's job is precisely that: to cut madness, mad karma, from the mind.)

Before the bell ending zazen and after the sound of the drum we place our *kesas* and *rakusus* on our heads and all together chant the *Dai Sai Geda Puku* (the kesa sutra) with hands in gassho. The dojo fills with the voices chanting in praise of the kesa transmitted from Buddha to the patriarchs, right up to ours truly in a straight unbroken line. Then we rise to our feet and begin the ceremony, the prostrations, the echo or prayer, mingled with the sound of the bell, the mokugyo and the big drum.

We go down three times, each time hitting our brains on the ground, same thing every morning, takes place directly after zazen, whatever brains we have left we leave behind on the floor, and go next door for genmai. This finished, everyone gets on with his own affairs, going where he will, and while some stay put with the master, his secretary, first disciple and Greta or someone else for the house-cleaning, others go off to the office, and yet others off to bed again and, as for myself, I go to the café on the corner and order a beer.

I try to think about the teaching this morning but have already forgotten almost everything. So I think of the teacher instead, which is easier. Too bad everybody doesn't have a teacher like Yakumatsu. Then everybody would

164

be like me, I mean like themselves, how great the world would be then!

Well it does no good thinking about the teacher either, gets you nowhere. Wiser to think about yourself, study yourself and forget yourself, this is the beginning of practice, any practice.

The teaching was very strong, very moving this morning. The master spoke of true mind and he said you should bring it to life: Build it into your daily life…

I order another beer thinking: now it's easy to build *that* into your mind during zazen but try building it into your daily life, well that's another story.

Suddenly I recall a passage I read in an Edward Conze book: "The outward signs of a good Buddhist are a calm demeanor, serene countenance, graceful walk, and good complexion."

Sure, that too is very easy… for some people, for those who behave naturally as good Buddhists should… But as for myself… with my bad record… why even today…, I mean all this practice and do I follow the precepts or do I not? Indeed I do not. But what the hell I am not the only one. If it's true that one must follow the precepts, then let's face it I am completely amiss and so is everyone else around here.

Poor old Yaku having to put up with the likes of us, of me… Now, I have been taking up the master's time… no doubt about it… while he could be devoting it to others more worthy than myself… to Professor Conze for instance who surely does more for the good cause without ever having even *seen* a master, than I ever could seeing one all the time. Here I am sitting in the great master's company taking up his time, his space, his teaching, taking everything even the whiskey to wash it down. I have incurred what they call the great debt, the great I.O.U.... to be paid back in blood corpuscles and bone marrow.

Well then again I dunno. Did I come here to add Buddhism to the list of things to do and of things to be? Hell no!

I pay for the beer and look at my watch 10 am time to get busy. Get practical. Keep your mind on the tangibles, don't think good, bad, right or wrong, be right here-and-now, put one foot in front of the other, get moving and don't look back.

Right at this moment I know what I am about, I am about to get divorced today. Today is divorce-day.

On my way to the Mairie, I think of Yaku my master, wondering what he would do... in fact wondering what he *did* do, or didn't do – in fact Yaku, whose wife was in Tokyo, didn't do anything at all. No, he just forgot about it...

Bah! What do I care what Yaku does with his life and besides it's none of my business – there are certain things in this world you don't question (let alone imitate or emulate), like for instance the private lives of other people, masters included.

So, as far as I am concerned, I am going to get the divorce now, before it's too late. Before they raise the price or change the law or something.

I arrive at the Mairie and wait, in the designated place, for the clerk. Monsieur? he addresses me. / Oui, pour l'aide judiciaire, legal aid, a matter of divorce. / Here fill this out, he slaps a form down in front of me.

I do as he says. Place of birth, passport number, place & date of marriage, name & middle name of parents, names & dates of dependents. Then a second page of questions concerning child support, alimony, employment – jobs held in the last 15 years, employers' names addresses and phone numbers – and finally a whole bit about weekly income, monthly income, stocks bonds property titles claims leases mortgages bank-numbers tax-receipts and sweepstakes profits.

I draw an X through the entire second page, all this has nothing to do with me, I'm running on empty, and the clerk, a skinny hardegg who has been watching me out of the corner of his eyes, sees the X on the second page and snaps the questionnaire in my face like he has been personally insulted or something, and he leans over the counter and looks at my wardrobe, Chevalier's jacket, Bernie's flannels, Stanley's shoes, and he looks at my face too, a white-skinned, blonde, blue-eyed Caucasian, and it is clear he doesn't believe me. He says: I see, and tell me please who is doing the providing? Is it your wife? Is it perhaps les petites dames, the little women?

I try to explain, this here was given to me by Bernie the pant salesman and this here... But what's the use telling him anything? He has it in his thick head that I am either a gigolo or a parasite, and he won't listen.

I have half a mind to grab the clerk and drag him over, change that smug face for him, put some terror into it, just for variety. But then again, who cares what he thinks. So I say instead: Yes, you are right, I am provided by friendly women – and men too – friendly people quoi.

Then you must write it down! He jabs his finger at the second page. I pick up the pen and write: friendly contributions. He snatches it up and walks away, and when he comes back he says: Please, the address where you were married. Write down the correct address please. / With the postal code number too? / Yes, yes, the complete address.

I know what he wants, to put a check out on me, see if I am really me. Well, it's no sweat off my ass, I am me alright and if he doesn't even believe that, who cares, he's paying for it not me. I take up the pen again and write down the correct address. Federal Courthouse, 100 Centre Street, that is the city prison, the Tombs, not the swankiest place to get married in, but it's legal alright, they have a pastor who sits in a back room and they even have organ music piped in, all by the books, and it goes very fast too.

And how do you pay your rent? asks the clerk.

Well I don't pay it.

You live in a rented room?

Yes.

Yes, then show me your *quittances*, your rent receipts.

The landlord doesn't give us *quittances*. No one in the entire building gets a *quittance*!

He lets you all live there for nothing? Come now!

You see he's a little… (I screw my finger to my temple and staring at him, I make a terrible face.) He's a veritable crackpot, ask anybody!

The clerk is taken aback. I nod my head and grin like a dog, showing my teeth and the clerk steps back. Maybe it's me the veritable crackpot, he thinks, maybe I am even dangerous, a terrorist maybe. But whoever I am, one thing is sure, I am too much trouble… Now sign your name here… Thankyou and good-bye!

When I arrive home, I open the door carefully (so it won't fall off) and what do I see? A mouse! No, not one mouse but two, three of them! It's the deluge. Bei Gott! I yell and at the same time swing at the closest with my unglued shoe.

Once upon a time not so long ago there was only one mouse. One mouse isn't so bad, you can have lots of human feelings when it is one mouse. But you kill it anyway, that's life. Whew! No more mouse. The critter is no more, you say, may he rest in peace, and me too while we are at it. Then comes another mouse – oh man, isn't there any peace around here? – well, you kill him too. There, no more mice! But as each day brings you another mouse to kill, the whole perspective changes, the innocent critter whose brains you have just crushed doesn't affect you so much, you don't chant anymore mantras and sometimes you even forget to do gassho when you drop him in the trashcan.

15

He was very strong, Rabelais, writer, doctor, jurist…
But he had troubles, the poor guy; even while alive,
he spent his time avoiding the stake.

L.-F. CELINE

"…Although these monks wrote books about zen and zazen," says the master, "they were only objective descriptions, or otherwise these books merely described morals and health according to their own reflections; these were works useful merely in making others quiet, peaceful or healthy…" (We rise up for kinhin, then sit back down again, and the teaching resumes.) "These monks did not go beyond the first step. Therefore they cannot teach and educate others, let alone transmit true zazen from person-to-person. So please, my dear disciples, in the future do not make the mistake of teaching in the fashion of these books."

Certainly books are only books, even the books of monks, but who cares, I go home and spend the rest of the day reading them anyhow… Here's one about 'American Zen' as they call it. Do you know that American Zen has bakeries and libraries and kindergartens and dojos and cafeterias and restaurants all over the place? Depressing stuff… Makes you wonder… Next book: "My Spontaneous Awakening" by Ms. Goldblatt the milkcow of zen – it's all about how zen people do it, how they maintain themselves on a higher level, eating vegetable dishes and drinking herb tea… Next the magazine called *New Age* – about positive thinking and… and by now I am left positively without a soul and feeling sick on top of it.

Well, never despair, when in doubt read Rabelais for a jolly good hour or two and the world will right itself again. Now here's a writer for you, such stories such fat stuff! Gargantua, the open-minded, non-sectarian, happy-faced giant, has a bladder of such proportions that when he pisses on the university, everybody has to put on their swimsuits and start paddling. And when he shits, the turds are so huge they turn into little pygmies and the little pygmies copulate and copulate and very soon indeed they grow into a rather prosperous little community, believing in God, going to church and all that…

Of course the theologians and the professors were quite put out by this rabble-mongering moron, and so they decided to burn his books. But this didn't work. The stupid people were buying and selling the stories on the black-market, it was like the dope market today, a real panic – why who knows, the way Rabelais was selling he would soon be outstripping the Bible in readership. So it was decided to hell with the books, they would burn him instead and good riddance.

It's 5 pm, time for a little fresh air, a walk, a stroll in the quarter, the Latin Quarter, the University, sure why not, go to see the statues. Maybe they have a Rabelais around there these days who knows.

Twilight and I am strolling along the cold cobble-stoned Rue des Écoles, Street of the Schools, mobes and bikes and scraggy people in dull-colored coats pushing by, and here on my left is l'Université de Paris, La Sorbonne, with its stony archway, stone walks, stone walls and all of it covered in the greyish slime of learning.

Lots of students talking, shouting, elbowing one another, talking about the world, talking truths, not made-up nonsense you talk about as you grow older.

I enter through the archway, a surprisingly narrow space when you think of it, not large enough to get much of anything through in one shot, just in trickles... And I am in the huge courtyard, the sky grim and humid, the Grand Amphitheatre, safe statues of Hugo and Pasteur; but no sign of Rabelais anywhere around this place.

Back on the Street of the Schools, the city of light, stumbling along under the polluted yellow streetlights, winding through the crowds of faceless faces, looking for the Rabelais statue I never find, no one wants Rabelais around today, didn't want him around much then either... like I said...

The man was last seen in Lyon. He was in shackles and heading for prison under escort, and no one heard another peep out of him again, that's for sure.

It all happened quietly and quickly. Rabelais was led through the prison doors, dragged off to the dungeon, dank and sour and lit by huge torches, a spit, a rack, a waterwheel, rubber hoses, whips, throngs, a thumbscrew and a newly invented wine-press contraption. The turnkey tore off Rabelais' robe, collar and codpiece, stuffed a dirty rag in his mouth and made him kneel down and cross himself before the cross (as was the noble custom). Then he reshackled the man to the centerbar inside the new-fangled wine-press. The turnkey nodded to the mean old turnspit, and the turnspit began turning the level, and the sound of crushing bones, mingled with the last gasps of the dying man, and with the cries of the officials – Long live the learned! Long live the universities! Long live God! – filled the dungeon.

So you can understand, no one was about to write up any decree or proclamation; now was the time for all God-fearing Frenchmen to keep their mouths shut... So you will find no statue, no slab, tablet, painting, drawing or sketch, no lycee no nothing named after him, not in this city at any rate. No obituary no necrology either, not in all the official annals anywhere.

But as far as word of mouth and word of writing goes, we have nicer things to say about old Rabelais today. I mean if you are, say, an assistant professor at one of the universities these days and you pick Rabelais for your study, you will surely be showing just the correct amount of courage and imagination required to be a good academic fellow. This is how it goes, first we castrate and castigate, then all together at the given moment in history when no one cares anymore, we magnify glorify and decorate the dead with dung. (And so it will be one day soon with Louis-Ferdinand Céline, another present-day affront to decent God-fearing French patriots.) I tell you lipservice is not lacking. Wind up the talking dolls please...

16

If I had to do this over again, I'd be a dentist or a barber.

BUKOWSKI

Huh what's that? That is the telephone and the telephone is on the floor... Who?... oh Caroline... what time is it... what day is it?... Sunday? Monday? ah Monday okay, it's okay today is hosan. No zazen no zaso. Monday for a monk is really Sunday for a Frenchman, and Sunday for a Frenchman is Monday for a monk. Some monks are happy when it's Monday because there's no zaso and they can do other things. But as for myself I am not so happy because me I never do other things, without zaso I am nothing, a lump on a log... Yes Michael! she almost shouts into my ear, Time to wake up! Then, in a subdued voice: May I come over?...

It's her lunchbreak again and seeing that I am just a hop-and-a-jump down the block, and being that I am not doing much of anything anyway, I say sure come on over!...and surely nothing brings a man-in-bed-doing-nothing more pleasure than to find a winsome lady standing overhead arms akimbo smelling of action in fur coat, black leather gloves, embroidered stockings and high boots for stomping...

Yes, very snappy indeed... hadn't much noticed my girlfriend before... maybe because of all the other girls and... Well anyway, I'm a lucky man. C. has it all, a nice body, a nice head, a nice wardrobe and a car to boot... That was a lucky break meeting her when I did, down in the dumps and drunk as a skunk... Had been drinking with Don, drank too much, staggered outside, flopped on the bench in front of the Coupole and fell asleep. Don't know how long I slept but when I woke up I noticed my coat had fallen off – for lack of buttons – and I was shivering (it was below zero weather). I picked up the coat which was about two sizes too large – found it in a trashcan no kidding, a gabardine trenchcoat and quite a nice one at that – and wrapped it about. It was then that I noticed someone staring at me, from inside a parked car. I stared back, it was a woman. The woman got out of the car and called to me, over the roof: Are you alright? / Alright? What makes you think I am not alright? / You were lying there with your coat on the ground. / Oh, yes. Un-hunh. / But I noticed it didn't seem to bother you very much. / Well I was sleeping, said I, straining my eyes to see what she looked like (it was around 2 am and quite dark out). How long have you been sitting there? / Well ever since I saw you lying on your back without your coat on. / Oh, so you just sat back and watched me without my coat on? / I came over and examined you, to see if you were alright. You know, I was amazed by your breathing, it was so deep, and also you looked so peaceful on that bench, without your coat on. / Atcha-atcha atchooooooo! I sneezed. / Would you like a ride somewhere? / Why not?

I opened the door on the curb side and slipped in beside her. She offered me a cigarette. I took in the smoke. The motor was running at idle and it was nice and warm inside.

How long have you been sitting here? I asked again. / Oh about ten or fifteen minutes, she said pulling out from the curb and pressing down on the accelerator. / Lucky I woke up, otherwise you might have driven off without me… We talked and looked each other over. Don't know what I looked like to her but she looked just right to me, her face just right, her legs just right… I watched the legs move up and down on the pedals and I thought maybe… maybe…

One pm and I am already wasted. She too. Too wasted to return to work, too wasted even to get out of bed. We smoke and say nothing much.

What day is the appeal? I ask. / Next Wednesday. I didn't sleep at all. / No, I can understand.

The thing is Caroline lost her child in a custody suit; her four-year-old boy Nicolas lives with his father down the block from her parent's pavilion in Antony, in the suburbs, and now she can't see him except on occasion, when the lawyer, and the father, decide it.

Okay let's do something! I jump out of bed, do a couple karate kicks, Let's get moving! Let's go to the movies! How much money you got? Good good. Look, there's this flick playing in Montparnasse, something to do with the life and loves of Charles the Terrible Bukowski.

On the way to the movie we run into Stanislas. Stanislas has some dope. So we head down the hill, smoking a joint. Then we split up and Caroline and I head for the movie. A flick about a down-and-out writer! Now this should be fun!

It's the big flick playing in Paris these days and it's no fun at all, in fact it stinks. Not the writer's fault, it's the Italian tamale of a director who's to blame. Why he's a real phony with no imagination at all. Sure, the down-and-out writer is no beauty, he needs a shave – his women need shaves too – and he goes about with a bottle of beer in a bland American suburb babbling poetry, but it's too much cold beer cold poetry and cold skinny women... I mean it's not fun to watch someone you respect being turned into an ugly no-class dildo covered in scabs and without teeth reading poetry to a bunch of old hags in a bland American suburb... why, what can you do, you have paid for your ticket – fifteen francs each! – and it's too late, no refunds sir.

Hey Caroline! I say on my way back from the cashiers, you like this thing?

Shhhhhh!

I sit down and look up at the down-and-out writer doing something stupid and I think, damn it, cornered again.

17

> To beg with your hands in your pockets makes a bad impression, it irritates the workers, especially in winter.
>
> BECKETT

I lift myself up on my elbows. Then crumble over. I try again. Ooof! Back up on my elbows. Shake my head. Three times. Once for the master, once for the sangha, once for the Dharma. Then just as I am about to sit up, Caroline grabs me by the neck… and down I go again for the count, down into the pit of nothing, like in zaso sometimes, and I am out… I wonder vaguely what's going on. Seems I was sleeping… then there was this jolt… like with one of those electric prods… you use on cattle… only in this case not on the hindquarters but right in the chakra… A spontaneous awakening… satori while you sleep… nothing to it…

I throw on my clothes, run down the stairs, run down the street, pass the meridianal-colored garbage collectors clanging cans like so many castanets, clinka-clank! clinka-clank! pass the squatters' stronghold all shuttered up in the good old Parisian soot, pass the sick old tree in the cold March dawn, counting the buds as I go – one-two-three – and I am in the dojo once again.

The monks and nuns are all old-timers today, Lucien Dagoba, Alphonse Lamponéon, René Manivel, Guillaume Tartaban, Georges Toutenbrosse, Joseph Baobab, Pascal Fardet, Viviane d'Armagnac, Emma Schweitzer, all with a load of years behind them, before them – I don't know – and we sit together, but I mean really sit, like a barn burning.

The bell rings and I am surprised, zazen seemed to last no more than five minutes and yet (I glance at my watch) and yet we've been sitting for one hour and twenty-three minutes without interruption.. There was no kinhin today, there was no kusen either. Yaku didn't show up this morning, there was no teaching and I hardly noticed!

Lamponéon conducts the ceremony this morning. Dressed in an old kolomo, a worn-out whitish kimono underneath, with headhair kind of shaved, Yaku's kotsu in his left hand, raggedy *zagu* on the tatami before him, Lamp)onéon drops down knees-first on the zagu three times running, once for the master etc., snatches the incense stick from Tartaban the kyosakuman, shoves it back to Tartaban the kyosakuman who in turn stabs it into the incense bowl while Lampjonéon burns shoko three times, once for the master etc., bows, does gassho, performs three more prostrations etc., all of this at supersonic speed – so that some of us, who are doing the same thing at the same time, are caught dropping down while others are popping up, and it's funny, sort of like Charlie Chaplin on the piano – and then the good and speedy monk, old Lampjonéon, shouts out the sutra –: Kan ji zai bo satsu! etc. – like all the devils do together and everybody has a good shout too… On our way out we stop before the altar on which sit the two statues (the plastic Buddha and Yaku's clay master Madawaki) place our palms together in homage and, frankly, it's a good feeling, let alone a good thing, to do homage to something or someone now-and-then, I think.

Back home I read my morning mail, a rendezvous with Monsieur Bonhomme my recently appointed legal-aid lawyer, and another rendezvous with my benefactor Chevalier who wants to give me money again I guess, when the phone rings –

It's Lee. We talk about this and that, about Yaku's health – Yaku wasn't with us in zazen this morning because, it seems, he is sick in bed. Something to do with his pancreas.

Say Lee, did you ever get that money from Yaku?

Yep.

No kidding. I sit down, cradle the phone between my chin and collarbone, and roll a cigarette. How much you get?

Ten grand.

Whew! Man you did it!

Well, he had me sign over the two cars as collateral. And if I don't pay him back by the thirtieth of next month, the cars are his.

And how much are they worth?

Together oh about fifty thousand, says he amused. Oh and by the way Old Bean, don't go and blab to anybody about this, you know what I mean?

Why? Cause others might try the same trick or some-thing?

Yes. And for other reasons. It might not look right to some people, you know… Lee and I wonder if a master should worry about his image. Should he behave as people expect him to?

We exchange current stories about masters in the States who don't look right, like the one over on the Coast who got caught red-handed doing the Mr. and Mrs. with one of his pretty little disciples. So what happened to him? He went up before the Board and got fired. No kidding. Then there was the one on the same Coast who had one drink too many and was sent to an asylum in a straight jacket. And about the other one on the other Coast who got caught with… well not with a girl… but with a boy – A BOY – in his bed. The Directors on this Board were positively horrified, of course; but they didn't have to fire this master – the disciples themselves handled that. They simply picked up their zafus and rushed out of the dojo, the pansies with their hands over their bungholes and the nunnies with their popguns plugged. The thing is, they are very virtuous over in America. *La vraie vertu quoi.* And they have good reason to be. I mean if you don't play it by the Cook Book over there, you will surely wind up cooked yourself – in carrot juice.

Think I will breeze off to the Sélect, have a fresh beer, foamy on top and wet below that. I count my money, five francs and fifty-five centimes left. Merde, not enough. Not like old Lee… ten grand…

I search through my pockets for some spare change just to make sure, and the whole while I imagine that the cameras are turning, I mean if it's really a movie I am living, then why worry, I might as well leave it up to the Director. Okay Director, what do I do next?

Do what you normally do! he shouts, for Christ's sake!

Hmmm? I scratch my head, a real imponderable. Well when I don't have anything more to do, says I, I beat my meat. You want I beat my meat?

No! None of that please! he shouts down at me from on high, we don't do pornography up here! Up here we do *true to life* stuff!

Work for that beer, clean a dish or two, sell your jacket-buttons, do a little panhandling. Like all you poets do. Sure, like Miller, like Burroughs, like Kerouac, Like Buk the Bastard.

Now he doesn't know what he's talking about. The last American panhandler was Jackie-boy London. London did it for years, begged all over, from the Niagara Falls to the Rocky Mountains and back again; he was real good at it, didn't mind putting himself where his heart was, not like me, me, I would rather die of thirst than beg for anything…

18

The master is away, directing a sesshin near Brussels. This man is always in zaso wherever he goes, and even when sick… So, there is no Yaku and no teaching, and yet the sitting is better than ever. Take myself for instance. I am sitting on this cushion so concentrated you can hit me on the head with a hammer and I won't know it. Now that's samadhi. Maybe not 'the frost-hail-wind-and-lightning' samadhi of the buddhas and the patriarchs, but it's a good one anyhow, you can hit me with a hammer, put a bullet in my brain, it doesn't matter… nothing will budge me no more…

(Reminds me of this monk I know, goes by the name of Lubberman. Lubberman was doing zazen early one morning in a park in Tangier. He was really going strong, sitting like old Mount Sumeru and all that, when this Arab happened by. The Arab looked Lubberman up-and-down and when Lubberman didn't budge once, he began to walk round him in circles. Then he threw a couple of stones at him. Still, nothing. So what the hell, the Arab stepped up and frisked him clean. It was a bad day for Lubberman, having lost his money, but it wasn't a bad zazen. I mean he didn't lift an eyebrow, he just kept right on going.)

So, as I was saying, we are sitting like all hell-fire and nothing will budge us… except maybe the bell.

I walk over to the café thinking about my latest mystical experience. Walking along the pavement, the croaking

183

tree on my right, a cement block with doors and windows to my left and the café up front. Pretty interesting. A rather unusual everyday walk, a rather unusual ordinary old café, and an unusual ordinary day, just like yesterday, just like tomorrow…

I mean just look at the sky this morning! it's actually clearing up! The layer of dishwater is disappearing right before my eyes, and everything is different. I mean just look at the women! the undulating gait… on wobbly heels… the ripple and flutter of cloth… the cute curtsies, ah the lovely unholy movement of it all!

The café is packed. Blue-collar types, zaso types. People are leaning on the bar drinking coffee and calvos and Dagoba and Plumo are playing the pinball machine and kicking it and banging it, and Ramon is sitting alone smoking a Gauloise, and Martinette and my old girlfriend the Queen of Sheba are talking about the *I Ching*, and my eyes rest on her face. The Queen ignores me, doesn't lift an eyebrow, but never mind, she has shaved her head this morning, nice and fresh and shiny and she is wearing a new colorful leather jacket with the fur collar pulled up about her neck and I observe her languid posture, airy grace and secret blush, all in one.

Time to see my divorce lawyer, Office on Avenue de l'Observatoire. I pass the statue of Maréchal Ney on the Place (erected exactly on the place where he was executed – by a bullet in the brain – or so my lawyer tells me) pass the Observatory (the place where you observe the cosmos through a telescope) dirty white-domed and forsaken… and I am in the office shaking hands with Mr. Bonhomme the legal-aid lawyer. Mid-thirties, gaunt, curly short black hair, and dressed in weather-beaten office grey. On the desk several piles of pocket-size bright-red books, penal and civil code stuff.

We talk about birth certificates, marriage certificates, divorce laws, legal aid and the cook book, himself leaning back on a swivel-chair, myself leaning back in an arm-chair, and one thing leads to the next and he asks me how in blazes do I make ends meet, the rent, the food, the café, and I don't know what to say anymore.

Next stop the Chevalier office, Rue du Départ. From one office to the next, from the Observatory to the Street of Departure.

I address the young lady who works in this office by her first name, Where's the boss this morning?... Well, the boss is busy elsewhere, but here, says Colette handing me a sealed envelope: This is for you.

I know what this is, it's the dough, the pudding. Before slipping the pudding into my pocket (the inside pocket near the heart) I check the pocket for holes, then from another pocket I pull out a bunch of pages, one, two, three, I count out ten pages, slap them flyswatter-like against the desk to flatten out the creases, slip them into a clean new envelope provided by the fine young lady in sweatshirt, jeans and heels, hand it back and sit down, on a stool, and fish about in my pockets for my tobacco and lighter which I find only after finding everything else – my rakusu, ID card, a pencil, a piece of paper with Mr. Bonhomme's address, a rubberband, a toothpick, a couple centimes. I roll a cigarette and she lights up a Marlboro and we talk about my writing (Colette does the photocopying and she is also one of my fans – says she likes my stuff because it's real "éclaté", which means something like exploded, blasted or busted) and then we wish each other a good day, kisses here and there, a little hug and a little squeeze, and I bust out for the elevator.

Counting the dough on the way downwards, one, two, three, four, five. Five hundred francs. That's fifty a page. Compliments of my benefactor. Ten bucks a page… Not much maybe, but then again what's enough? what's not enough?…

Be this as it may, the weather is rather balmy today. The sun is presently at its apex and it boils away the microbes and other microcosms in all ten directions. The old bellyaches and other things are boiling away and the people are all rather glad about it. Even the sparrows in the trees above the market, at Edgar Quinet, are hopping one over the other, wiggling their tails and chirping up a storm reminiscent of monks and nuns coming out of the long winter retreat at the café Le Métro, Plumo and Dagoba and Ramon and Martinette and the Queen of Sheba, and I count them – the birds – seventeen in all. Had to count twice.

So the food market is full to popping, all kinds of hawkers all kinds of food in all kinds of colors, golden apples, reddish radishes, yellowish bananas, pinkish pumpkins, orange oranges, purple pears, violet vinegar, brown beans and green-grown mint leaves.

Mint leaves! Didn't my neighbor Marianne Gottlieb the clodo-poet tell me that if you stick fresh mint leaves in the cracks and crannies, the mice will dash for cover forever, that's how much they hate mint leaves. Well, I buy 500 grams of mint leaves, a bushel of apples, bananas all of a baker's dozen and all this for 43 francs and 50 centimes, and first thing I do back home is stuff the entire 500 grams in the cracks and crannies, and sit down and watch. Nothing. I eat an apple and wait.

I try to write. A new day for new confessions… Not so easy though… Feeling a bit down suddenly. Must be this Yaku thing on my mind… just the thought of it… too hard to contemplate… no Yaku anymore? Come on, that's impossible… Better I think of my own life, what I myself am doing, about my writing, about the editors.

I think of all the editors who have read my stuff and hated it and it makes me kind of hate them too, of course. I pull out a letter from the Editor-in-Chief Mrs. So-and-so at Grove Press and read it over. You know, this dingbat here enjoins me to never send her anything I ever write in my whole life. It says so right here, signed by the Chief and all…

I just can't make her out. What kind of business is she running I would like to know… I tell you editors will haunt me right to the grave. I mean reactions like this one can really change a man's perspective. He can even lose it completely if he's not careful. Like what if they are right and I am wrong after all? Like what am I doing anyhow, doing something really so worthless? Like I am born for what, O Lord, to produce words no better than turds right to the grave?

By now I am pretty unhappy. Getting ready to write again I guess. Now why is that? why, because a happy man has nothing to write about. This is why real writers today laugh on the wrong side of their mouths. It not only gives them something to say, it also gives them something to do, like learn to laugh on the right side maybe.

Knock! knock! / Who's there? / It's me. / So it's you. / Am I disturbing you? / No, I am already disturbed as it is. Oh and by the way, I say glancing at my watch, I have a date with Caroline. For dinner.

It's my wife and she throws off her coat, kisses me right on the mouth, and right off she asks me about the divorce:

Are you really serious about getting this divorce?

Sure, *pourquoi pas*?

Have you seen the lawyer yet?

Yep.

Oh why are you doing this to me? she says in a beseeching voice beset, as they say, with feeling.

Look, Bonhomme is a good guy and he will get it for us for nothing. This is our chance. Any day now they're going to change the laws, so let's get it now while we can, I mean can you see us bound and chained together throughout eternity just because we didn't have the money or because the laws changed or because –

Why do you always talk nonsense? Whenever a situation becomes serious all you do is prattle nonsense.

Lydia goes into the kitchen, helps herself to a glass of water, returns and sits down on my bed, right at home.

When my parents die, she says, we will have some money and then we can be together again, like before.

Come off it. Anyway it could be years maybe even a decade before the Devil takes them away, I mean God of course, and so you see who's talking nonsense around here? "When my parents die" – you should be ashamed of yourself!

They are both in their mid-seventies, she continues not a bit ashamed of course, They are both sick and weak and I tell you they will not last much longer.

Now of course it's better to love one's parents, I am thinking, and to hope that they will live forever and forever. This notwithstanding, it certainly is soothing to think along these other lines, a person needs a little hope of his own, something to lift the morale, something to warm the heart and a little death or two along with a respectable inheritance and a second little honeymoon can't do anyone any harm as far as I can tell.

We sit quietly hand in hand with emotions soft as swans, like in the good old days, when we had money, when the telephone rings.

Don't answer it Michael.

I answer it anyway. Curiosity… (Curiosity killed the cat, but in this case it killed him twice, as we shall soon see.)

It's Caroline, I say cupping my hand over the phone. She tells me she's on her way over… No not right now, I say into the phone. Yes I'm busy right now… Yes, busy… Busy at what? Busy at my Buddhism. Yes that's right. Come over in about let's see come in about half an hour say. I hang up.

THANKS ALOT ! Lydia screams at me.

I told you I have a date with Caroline for Christ's sake.

Your *Buddhism*! Look who should be ashamed of himself!

Huh huh huh! And what do you think Buddhism is anyway? BUDDHISM IS NOT ON ONE SIDE, I shout back, AND LIFE ON THE OTHER, for Christ's sake. It's not a museum around here!

Well, you don't have to go and lie about it! Why didn't you tell her the truth?

I didn't want to tell Caroline the truth because then maybe she wouldn't fuck me tonight, but I don't admit that to Lydia.

Sometimes, I explain patiently, sometimes you must use expedient means, no point in hurting people. *Expedient means*, you know what that means? Listen to what I am going to tell you… This said, I recite a passage from the *Vimalakirti Sutra* on expedient means.

So the good Buddhist, she snaps at the end of my recitation, is rushing me out of here in thirty minutes, is this what I'm to make out of this Vamakuchi –

No, twenty minutes now, I say interrupting her and looking at my watch.

Lydia dresses, not a word, just the sound of clothes being thrown about, lots of violence in the air… Once dressed she grabs her coat and storms out. I jump up and catch the door before she slams it. Last time it fell off the hinges…

Whew, she's gone. I look at my watch. Man, let me tell you, the superfluous woes of daily life can knock down the best among us…

Knock, knock, it's Caroline… I catch my breath, inhale, exhale and open the door. Bonjour ma chérie, I kiss her hand, Come in and make yourself comfortable. My but that's a *new* dress you are wearing, isn't it?... I give her my hand and holding it over her head she turns about like in a minuet for two. The dress is white and rather tight and… and I enter the kitchen and return with a bottle of wine and two clean glasses.

C. holds up her glass and I fill it up, so sexy so soft and curvy in her tight white dress and frankly I wouldn't mind filling her up too and not just with wine juice… But wouldn't you know it, the lady doesn't want it other than in the glass today, she's got other things on her mind and she says, speaking of her child, of Nono, over in the banlieu: All this arguing and fighting and Nono is right in the middle of it! It's not his fault! Why he will only be five in June!

I want to tell her to shove it with her kid – Nono, it's the perfect name – but I contain myself and think instead of what it must mean to Caroline. They have taken away her child… and now my thoughts are not just on Caroline, but with all the mothers in the world who have had their little Nonos taken from them… and then I think of all the little Nonos who have gone and lost their mothers, Nonos like myself for instance, and I shake my head and suck my knuckles in despair.

I reach for the bottle and pour two glasses full to the top. C. swallows it down in one gulp, then: May I call them on your phone?

I listen vaguely to the conversation and wonder at the same time if this isn't what may be in store for myself (and my own wife and child) very soon whatwith our own divorce going through and all, I mean all that about visiting rights and…, and C. is shouting into the phone: LET ME SPEAK TO NONO!

I get up, walk into the kitchen close the door and open the faucets. But you can still hear them going at it, even the father shouting over in the banlieu, and that's how the phone call ends: SALOPE DE MERDE! I'LL KILL YOU! Then the distant crash of a phone being dashed to the floor, and the nearby bang of my own phone being slammed down, BAM!

I try to soothe things over, you know listen to her stories about that bastard in the banlieu, see that she is comfortably seated, make her fresh coffee with lots of sugar and an apple to go with it, and I put in a word or two myself – it'll be alright Caroline! You'll see! etc. – but unable to convince her of this, I give it up. Meanwhile C. works herself up into a lather and flings the apple against the wall where it sticks, and I can't take much more of this, I mean when you're in an air-raid you hit the deck, when you're in a cyclone you head for the eye, and this being the case, I pull my rakusu out of my pocket, sling it over my head and sit down, on the floor, under the apple still on the wall.

Anyway, it helps everybody, even her.

7 pm and we are on our way to the banlieu. It was decided that we would visit Caroline's childhood friend, Jerome, now living in Issy-les-Moulineaux. Change the scenery.

We take the metro and we walk. She points out a window on the second floor of a quaint two-story house with a curlicued iron gate out front and says, That's the place.

Inside kind of quaint too. Stuffy teddybears on the chairs, puffy snowballs on the walls, a smug rug, a counterfeit couch, a deficient three-legged table and matching lampshades made in Taiwan. Jerome is around twenty and he too is kind of quaint, a kind of combination between Peter Pan and a boneless jellyfish. His friend Loulou though is another matter. He is about sixteen and could be vicious, if contradicted. I take a moment to look him over. He's the kind you don't see around for long, he's either in jail on a life stretch or otherwise he's already dead. Society can do without the likes of him, shove him in prison and good riddance.

So Loulou is sitting on the fake couch his feet up on the three-legged table smoking cigarettes and flicking them half-finished on the smug rug with Jerome politely picking them up one by one behind him.

We get to talking and he tells me he's here on a holiday... On a holiday? I ask. What are the other days like when you're not on holiday?

When I'm not on holiday I'm in the cage.

In the what?

He means the Juvenile Detention Home, cuts in Caroline. He's here on a two-day holiday.

Oh? I turn back to Loulou, And where's that?

Lyons.

Lyons, I mumble. Whenever I hear the name Lyons I think of Rabelais. People there were really nice to François Rabelais in Lyons, they were.

They gave me two days to see my pote my pal… Loulou points with his thumb: He signed the papers.

You in charge of him? I ask Jerome who is busy picking up a butt. Ha that's a good one, I think to myself. I can see it, Jerome getting buggered in the ass by Loulou, that's how much he's in charge of things around here… Loulou, I say, have you any family, a mother or a father?

Yes I do, says he, and I don't care if I never see 'em again. The feeling's mutual.

And how's life in the cage treating you?

Oh alright. Then, more thoughtfully: They always keep you busy cleaning the latrines and the floors and things. You're always with a mop and pail in the cage. I've spent the best years of my bloody life mopping floors.

And the other guys? You get along with them?

They're alright, he shrugs and flicks a butt onto the floor. See this nose? Some guy broke it with an iron pail. See this here scar? See these stitches? That's from a broken broom handle. It's like this with everybody. It's the price you pay. Like paying your dues. To be a man in this world you gotta fight all the time, at the drop of a hat.

We leave the improbable people in the improbable house and here we are in the street in the night, no one, not a car, bike or pedallo, not a light on nowhere, everybody's asleep, counting sheep in fairyland… and Jerome and

194

Loulou…? I take C. by the arm, wondering if those two boys aren't going to be buggering each other in the quiet night perchance…?

We get off the metro at Montparnasse, that is we get off the RER at the Montparnasse train station, a kind of city within a city, and then we are crossing La Place Bienvenüe full of people bienvenue for their last shekels on the weepy end of a worn-out weekend at the café Rip-Off. Not the Montparnasse Hemingway wrote about… We hit the Sélect for a last unselective drink, two glasses of beer at the bar… It's been a tough day, feeling down, divorces and child stuff and all that… We have gone a long ways today, starting with the samadhi in the morning and finishing with the naraka in the evening… Oh well, we make the best of a bad deal, sitting at the bar, sipping our beers and tickling each other and talking nonsense… when someone sticks me in the ribs. Hmm? Don't know the guy, not Hemingway at any rate. I turn back to my beer. He sticks me again, with his elbow it would seem. I let it pass. He does it again – now that makes three times goddam it. Well, I'll just sit it out, like we do in the dojo what… but what if he sticks me again?... He sticks me again. I turn on my stool and look at him. He has a fat ugly face with little rat eyes, not the type you like to see much, and I say, Yeah?

I would like to talk to you.

Yeah well I don't want to talk to you.

He drags on his cigarette, like he plans to burn it into a butt in one big suck, and blows the stinking stuff right in my face.

All I really want in life is to be kind and gentle, but I must be fit enough to walk to the dojo tomorrow morning, not find myself going in a wheelbarrow, and I know I am going to take him because I am going to hit first and I am looking at his fleshy jawbone getting it all lined up when I'll be damned, if he doesn't turn away his jawbone in the nick of time to follow it straight across the bar and out the door.

So much for the Sélect tonight, so much for Montparnasse, not what it used to be, not like what Hemingway and Henry wrote about, drinking pastis and talking fancy. Now we drink piss and talk pasta around here… We walk past the Dome where Lenin and Trotsky used to hang out, now packed with African tribe-types, Arabian con-artists, Jewish shekel-faces and pink-skinned pansies with hangy asses, and past the late-hour pharmacy through which door Stanislas comes a-stumbling. He hasn't seen us and he bumps along the walls removing little brown bottles – probably paregoric – from a paper bag and distributes them into various pockets, to spread out the bulges. He crumples the bag and drops it on the pavement and I notice his shoes without laces covered in mud and dogshit, and suddenly I am feeling better.

Hey, Stanislas, what's up?

What! he jumps out of his skin, Ah it's you, oh just some medicine for my stomach, you know… Stanislas goes on to say something about playing the piano at the Closerie Piano Bar later tonight and he wants us to accompany him there… No, no, I have had it, and besides don't much like the Closerie Piano Bar, that prissy place full of cultivated

196

types in tweeds and smoking pipes and talking like they know something special there… No I don't want to go there…

Stanislas tries out Caroline, he can't face himself alone the poor wreck and he slips his arm about C.'s waist and turns on the charm. Tells her how pretty and intelligent she is, and it's good for her to hear, doesn't hear it much from me you can bet… and I watch them walk off toward the lights, he in his shitkickers without laces she in her fur coat and snappy high boots… Ah I must be getting old…

19

With a permit-running card in my fist I feel
like… I've hardly got a stitch on and am sent
against the frozen fields in a shimmy and
shorts.

> A. SILLITOE, *The Loneliness of the Long-
> Distance Runner*

"Hello," the bird said, larfing too
"I hope you don't mind me
I've come to guide you here on in,
In case you're lost at sea."

> J. LENNON, *In His Own Write*

I lie in the dark listening to the humming of the fridge.
I scratch myself absentmindedly and wonder if it isn't the
bugs… sure, like that time down in Barcelona – Lydia and
I had to burn all our clothes… walked around in rain-
coats…

I throw back the quilt and flick on the light. Merde!
Nothing worse than light, sometimes. I mean there are
these bumps, little red things, all over my legs and thighs
– infection! disease! I grab my glasses and look for the
bugs… Hmm, don't see any… Good morning Caroline! /
What time is it? she mumbles. / Six-oh-nine, I've gotta go!
/ Oh skip it for once darling, and stay with me in bed. /
No, I've gotta go…

I jump out of bed. Gotta go to the pharmacy while I'm
at it… and to the cleaners. Wouldn't want to burn all my
nice clothes… I think about my clothes, particularly about

my pants... the striped ones, my flannels... my jeans.. One, two, three... I count to eight, no to nine. Nine pair of pants. Not bad. I open the curtain, grab the pants and shove them into plastic bags. Direction dry cleaners. Merde alors, no more pants left. Well, I can wear my kimono. My very first kimono... now old and faded...

The trip to the dojo this morning isn't so easy going. Almost don't make it. I mean the people you chance upon knocking about at six... Like the CRS, the Compagnie Républicaine de Sécurité. Over one hundred strong. No kidding. And all in formation. In columns extending from the buildings on one side of the street to those on the other. Blocking up the works. No one can get through.

I stop in my tracks and wonder, what's cooking? A putsch? A revolution?

Where are you going, Monsieur?

I turn around and see this face looking at me from under a raised visor. Stenciled on the helmet, over the eyes, is the word "Capitaine"... The Capitaine's question throws me off balance, so I just shrug and mumble incoherently.

Better you go back home, says he, looking me over from head to foot, at the two plastic bags, my kimono, my legs and my feet in shoes, without socks.

Ah bon, I mumble. / And get out of that dress while you're at it. / This is not a dress, I point out in passing, This is a kimono. / A what? / A ki-mo-no. A kind of djellaba. Tell me Captain, what's going on? What's the trouble? / The Squatters! And do not speak so loud! Do you want to wake them up?!

Ah, I get it now, the CRS devils wish to catch the squatters in their sleep and beat their brains out. Yes and maybe mine into the bargain. Maybe it would be a good idea to call it quits today, go home and take it easy… I turn and head homewards, thinking as I go that it doesn't matter if I do zaso or not today. Did it yesterday and will do it tomorrow, but today… No one will know the difference… except maybe if I end up in the hospital for six months somebody might say "Hey that Dilly-Dalley is a real pushover farting around in bed and all" while all along the doctor has me strapped down for a lobotomy…

Oh hell's bells! Am I a monk or am I not? I mean anyone on the Way knows it's the action that counts. Gyoji! The Eightfold Noble Path! Right action, right effort, right perseverance…

When I get to the first column I flatten myself against one of the buildings, the pharmacy building to be exact, and begin to side-step. I push past the fellow who is standing at parade-rest, his elbow about three inches from the building. I glance at his face in passing. Nothing there… And now I am in the middle of the whole thing and about to wedge my way through to the next column, when someone grabs me by the shoulder. Hé, Monsieur! / Oui? I turn around, it's the Captain behind his raised visor again. / Didn't I tell you to go home? / Ben oui, I grin back. / And get out of that dress?

The others standing about, in their uniforms, eyes forward, chuckle in their visors. I ignore the poor man and look at my watch. Time is running short at about the same speed as my patience is running thin, noble Eightfold Path or not… Now the Captain is poking one of my bags with his billyclub and I look down at the billyclub, which is wrapped in black leather, sort of like the gong-handle at the dojo, and good for beaning people like him, and we start one of those mundane conversations:

What are you carrying in there? he asks. / In here? Just pants, mon Capitaine. / Pants? Whose pants? / My pants, biensûr. / Let me see. / See? Pants. I open one bag and then another and the Captain pokes the pants about with his club. / Just pants? How many pairs? he asks real quick. / Nine pairs sir, I reply just as quickly. / What are you doing with nine pairs of pants, would you mind telling me that? / I am taking them to the dry-cleaners if you don't mind. / At this hour? No cleaners are open at this hour. Non Monsieur, you take me for a fool, don't you?

The situation is turning sour. Best I split. Go round the block or something… No quicker thought than done, I take off like a dart, in the direction of least resistance, back towards home; no one is behind me and I dart around the block, and am on the Rue Vercingétorix chopping wind like mad, the kimono hoisted up over my knees – sort of like running in your underwear but never mind – and now I am back on the Rue Losserand, that is back where I started though approximately one block south of my original point of departure, and I stop for breath and just then I hear this bellow right out of *Ben Hur* and the earth wobbles on its axle and here they come boy! Like black mud flowing down a funnel…

I get to the dojo looking like the black mud got me, step right in, bow to the Buddha and assembly combined, and grab a seat. No time to clean up, no time to change robes, I just sit there huffing and puffing and the bell rings and everyone stops what he's doing, everyone except me (you don't stop huffing and puffing at the drop of a hat you know) and the guy to my right goes SSSHH! right in my right ear.

I get the breathing back to normal by speeding up the lung movement – a kind of panting – and now with the fresh oxygen pumping through my blood vessels, the breathing is flowing nice and slow-like. I loosen up the stomach muscles, lower the *ki*, the energy center, to some-where below the navel, and now I get the head irrigated and flowing right nice too – by pulling on the backbone – and with the twenty-seven or so joints in the vertebrae unlocked and apart, the current circulates in one steady flow from the coccyx right up to the cockpit and back again... and now no more thoughts... no stagnation... no nothing...

Sweat is rolling off my chin and landing in the palm of my open hand... no big deal... I vaguely watch this drop roll off my nose. It lands plunk! in the puddle... Another drop, same thing... Here comes a third drop... rolls real slow... rolls right up to the tip... and stops dead. I twitch my nose but it's glued to the spot. I twitch it and twitch it, *are you gonna drop off or what*? I push out my lower lip and blow hot air upwards. Nothing doing. I shake my head... ah? what's that? Oh it's the kyosakuman tapping me on the shoulder. He wants to hit me. So be it, I turn my head to the left and while he hits me on the right shoulder I wipe the left side of my face on my left shoulder, then I turn my head to the right and he hits me on the left while I wipe off the right.

I have this crazy desire to scratch myself. It's the bugs… Well I overcome the temptation by sitting with my back stiff as a billyclub and my mind between my eyes, sort of reminiscent of that ink drawing of Rinzai sitting with teeth gritted, fists clenched and eyeballs a-popping…

…There's a bug strolling around in my underwear. I follow his peripathy, like the followers of Aristotle who walked about in the Lyceum while he was teaching, peripatizing lackadaisically round my crotch, up and about my navel, then down my left leg to the knee… Huh, I don't feel him anymore… Wonder where he went… Ah there he is! On the hem of my kimono. He's on top of the hem and I can actually see him. That's how big he is. He advances by the hop. Little wings batting. Must be of the flea species… Ooops! he hops onto my knee… ooops he hops onto my neighbor Bombaclou… Ah, another one. Almost the size of a beetle. He hops off to join his pal on my neighbor, Bombaclou… Here's another… and another and another and I take a swat at the closest one and the kyosakuman shows up again and takes another swat at me and that does it, they are jumping off like rats on a sinking ship… Man if this thing keeps up the whole house will be hopping soon. Hehe… Sure, and everybody will be monkey-scratching and dousing themselves with flea powder… and boiling their kimonos and cooking their underwear… and too they'll have to burn the curtains and empty out the zafus and fumigate the rug… Well, I was just following the Noble Eightfold Path, and it is thanks to its application at the right moment, that is in the heat of action and precisely at that moment when I almost became resigned, and in a most apathetic manner – I was about to go back home as you will remember, my two bags of bugs and my tail between my legs – why like I say, it's thanks to the application of the true teaching that I even got here to the shrine in the first place! So if anyone blames me about the bugs in the dojo I will just say it was Beauneveu the garbage collector who brought the bugs not me! Now, what's a good garbage collector if he doesn't have the bugs to prove it…

There goes another bug. Just hopped onto Bocalo's head. Some people have heads on top of their heads, at least this is what Rinzai says, but Bocalo the philosopher has a bug, hehe.

Suddenly it dawns on me. The whole thing, everything, is in my head! Everything is makyo!... While most people go about seeing buddhas and bodhisattvas everywhere, other people, people like me maybe, go about with their heads stuck in the back of a garbage truck…

I am about to start zaso when the bell rings. One hour down the drain. How many hours have there been… like this… during the past ten years… sitting here… picking bugs…?

I borrow a pair of pants from Bernie the pant-man, drop off my own at the cleaners and head for the pharmacy. Show the lady my bumps. She gives me some ointment to be mixed twice before spreading three times a day or something and I look her over and her grey hair is practically sticking straight up on her head, her body quaking at the knees, and I ask her what's the matter. Is it my bumps a-scarifying you so much? to which she replies, Oh no, it's the squatters across the street. / Oh that bunch of bums, I smile relieved it's the bums and not the bumps. They say in the newspapers they were a bunch of heroin addicts, is that right? / That's what the papers said, says the woman with a kind of Oriental understanding in her face – she's Vietnamese. The papers say it was heroin, but it was Elixir Parégorique that bunch were taking. And if anyone should know it's me.

I think of Stanislas who is on that paregoric stuff himself and I wonder if it isn't this Vietnamese lady who sells him the stuff. How do they get the stuff, I ask, Do they need a prescription? / No, she hands me back the change, they don't need a prescription, they don't even need any money anymore to get the stuff. They got all their Paregoric from me. In the end they weren't even paying for it. They just stole it. / They stole it? When you were in the back? / In the end they stole it right in front of me. Even while I was looking.

I am in the street feeling sorry for the old lady and thinking how tough it gets for the old and the weak, when I see some squatters being herded, handcuffed, into a waiting van.

Going to jail, I suppose, I say to the fellow next to me on the curb. He looks at me curiously, then: You don't send those types to jail, that would create problems. They're off to Barbès. The CRS truck them out of Montparnasse and dump them off at Barbès-Rochechouart, my friend. Where they belong.

Up there with the Bougnouls, I nod to myself… It's actually only a question of real estate. I mean who owns this place? well *they* don't at any rate, so let's get them out of here what…

I turn to watch the action. The last of the vans pulls out, a fire truck out front turns off the water, two bulldozers in the yard shove the garbage around, and lots of men in blue go in and out of the house, and through the windows or what's left of the windows – just big black holes – you see the demolition men busy at work.

I watch this demolition man on the third floor shove a big dripping mattress through one of the holes. The mattress is full of water and it hits the garbage out front with a dull schlop! and someone in the crowd says with awe, They hosed that Bougnoul while he was still in bed!

Just then a crane looms up out of nowhere, lifts off the roof and throws it away. My God let's get out of here! Well what's a man to do? That's the law. Oh I know the law okay. You can always find good things in the law, if you try hard enough. It keeps the streets clean and the people good. Even the street lights have their goodly qualities. Like right now we arrive at the corner and we look up at the light, and if it's red we stop, do gassho and meditate. Meditate on the red do kinhin on the green… Anyway, that's how they do it in some zen places. The master gives you what he calls a koan, a kind of hard problem even Einstein can't solve, and he says: You must solve this problem. Now to solve this problem you must concentrate. Concentrateconcentrateconcentrate…. So you work on this problem all the time, not only while you sit but also while you eat and drink and piss and shit and cross the street. And if you are at this moment concentrated on the curb like nobody's business and a cross-eyed truck driver flattens you in the middle of your koan, you can always scream gaaaaahhh!

I sit down in my chair, roll myself a joint and relax. Been a tough day... so far... and not yet 10 am... and I think of the squatters, of those guys who used to sit out on the stoop and smoke dope, just like me right now... and then I think of the mice. I check out the traps, no trace of a mouse in this place dead or alive. Guess the mint works after all... I unhook the traps and fling them on a shelf, no more killing for this boy, sit down at my desk, which really isn't a desk but a board on trestles, do gassho and write: The alarm goes off announcing a new day and I fart and fart and –

What? Who the blazes! Why it's another mouse! Coming across the floor, Hey, he's coming right at me! He hops over my foot and scurries up the slanting trestle-leg, stops about three feet from my face, squats on his hind legs on the page and stares at me with his black beady eyes. We stare at each other for a bit and then, as if completely at home here in my house, he begins cleaning his snout with his paws... I get up and retreat to the kitchen, for an instrument. I pick up the meat-knife and think, if I move fast enough I can cut him right now, while he cleans his snout.

I observe him through the door... A strange mouse, takes over my room, takes over my desk, has me crouching in the kitchen with a knife, doesn't give a damn if he lives or dies… All this makes me wonder… I mean what's he up to? What's he doing on my paper? Is he going to shit hieroglyphics on the page for me to decipher later? I step up and hold the knife over his head, about to chop it off… But do you think he cares? No, he just goes on picking his snout… Like master Raisan, busy with his potato while the executioner takes aim at his throat… but that's another story… I place the knife under his throat, right on the jugular vein. Okay mouse, you are going to die!

He cleans out one nostril, then the next. He must be crazy. Or maybe it's just dope, like too much mint or something. I study his face… Sure enough he's bananas. You can tell by the bloodshot eyes, by his grey complexion, by the strange little hairs all over his skin, by the way he keeps scratching himself, by the way he keeps moving his buck teeth up and down, by the way he keeps twitching his snout, like he's been sniffing coke lately. Twitch twitch. Hey cut that out!… He looks at me, steps a little closer, right up to my face in fact, and twitches… Ah maybe it's just a sign of affection, maybe he likes me, maybe he wants to kiss me. That's it, everybody is always kissing me, I am loved by everybody, the bugs and mice included.

He hops up on my typewriter. Hey mouse, I say, why don't you type out a little jingle while you're at it mouse?

Why certainly Boobha! he replies, to my great surprise. Not only can he speak… but also he called me by my official ordination name, Boobha… Anyway, before I know what's happening, he hops about on the keyboard and composes a fine little jingle into the bargain:

While I was in the human house
I taught you to catch many a mouse
and now whatever you do Boobha
be sure to catch a buddha

"Say that's pretty good for a spaced-out mouse. Look, I don't know how you learned my ordination name, but around here we don't go by such fancy tags. So you can forget the Boobha business and just call me Mike, Mike the Knife, okay?"

"Okay Boobhalubah, and you can call me Bodhisattva Spaced-Out."

"You a bodhisattva? Come off it, you're just a dumb mouse anyone can tell that."

I stick him with the knife and the mouse hops sideways and says, "If me just a mouse you just Al Capone."

"I'm a different Al Capone," I reply, "I don't eat you afterwards." "Yes, right in the trashcan," says he, "no ceremony no nothing. You was bad to no end but it's your birthwrong to fall right with Bodhisattva Spaced-Out."

"Oh come off it, who's ever seen a bodhisattva in a fur coat tell me that?"

"Hawhaw, this no fur coat, Stupido, this my monk robe"…

20

No zazen today, Hosan. Holiday. Goof off. Take it easy, don't do anything. Don't answer the phone, don't talk to anybody, the mice included. Well, good luck! I am sitting at the desk drinking wine and reading a book by Chandler, when suddenly the door opens and in walks Stanislas, without knocking… You can knock next time… He ignores me, walks directly up, slaps a folded newspaper down on the desk and says: Look at this!

I don't look at it, I look at him. His fly-zip is bust open. That's a nice pair of pants you're wearing, I observe.

These pants cost me five francs at the flea market! he snaps. Now, look at this, he jabs the paper with his finger.

I glance at the article. It's about the police bust down the street. Yeah? So what?

So what? he repeats. Read it and you'll see.

I read it. Something about a tip-off. The squatters were on the point of receiving a shipment of heroin, but thanks to the tip-off, the cops caught them red-handed, or almost. The Commissaire learned of the impending transaction from a certain un-named North African who was an insider on the deal… I look up, The usual thing, so what?

The usual thing? héhé. Stanislas laughs diabolically, rolls himself a cigarette from some tobacco on the desk, spills the stuff all over, puffs furiously, points at the article and says: See this bit about the rat, the stoolie? Well, that's me. / That's you? / Ben oui ben oui, he nods proudly. I ratted on them night before last, tipped off the cops on the shipment. / The shipment? / Ben oui the shipment. / And how did *you* know about it? / About what? About the shipment? That's just the point, *there was no shipment*. / What do you mean there was no shipment? You just said – / What I just said I made up, he says.

What? You mean to tell me… what you just said… look here Stanislas… (I am on the verge of throwing him out, nothing I hate more than gibberish)… You don't understand a thing. I was the rat alright, but that bit about the shipment, I made up that part, I invented it! Now let's have a drink… I pour Stanislas a glass of wine. So you invented it. Well, go on… Stanislas picks up the phone and says: See, I am in the phonebooth on Rue de la Gaîté and I am talking to the Commissaire in Bougnol language… Stanislas does the impersonation of an Arab, giving a detailed description of the shipment and the hour of delivery and all that. Stanislas has got a score to settle with the squatters on Losserand, they burned him once too many… And they believed you? I ask somewhat doubtfully.

Ben la preuve, the proof, he replies sitting down on the floor. He pulls his dirty pants neatly up over his boney knee-caps, crosses one leg over the other and goes on: They knocked down the floors and tore up everything you ever heard of, didn't they? Why they believed me alright. / Why did you do it, Stanislas? / Hey you have any more wine? / No, that's the end of it. / I know you have more you are just hiding the bottle cause you are a cheap S.O.B… This said, he stumbles into the kitchen and stumbles back with the bottle… Well, go on with the story. Why did you do it? / I already told you, I made it up… He puts the bottle to his lips. / Alright alright! Why did you do it, why did you make it up? Why did you squeal on the squatters? Why did you call the cops you worthless human wreck? / Okay, I did it, just like that. For nothing. I had one franc left and I thought to myself, let's see how far we can make one franc go.

I observe him. His shirt is torn and held together with one button, his shoes with rubberbands; he has no socks and no underwear and you can see his thin elongated cock through his fly which, as I said, is bust, and his eyelids are red and swollen from the paregoric and little balls of spit bubble at his lips, and he tells me about the old lady who runs the pharmacy down the street and he says that the poor old lady didn't dare go home at night whatwith all those awful people shaking her down for the paregoric. They cleaned her out every morning at nine. And in the end, he says, the tears running down and mingling with the bubbles of spittle at the corners of his mouth, She didn't have a single bottle left.

21

A white man carefully puts coal on the fire and steps back toward a giant door which seems to lead somewhere else.

J. LENNON

The time is half-past-six on the kwatz and everyone is awake, myself included. It's dim and dusty outside and there's no good reason to get out of bed, let alone to be awake…, and yet there's this suspense in the air – or is it in life I dunno – and I walk sprightly along the street, past the pile of garbage (the squatters' stronghold or what's left of it), past the restaurant Le Breton (where Caroline and I celebrated our honeymoon) and, by god, the house is packed this morning. Must be that Yaku is back. Ah so, Yaku was the suspense and his reappearance is the good news. Sure thing I love that man, don't know exactly why…, so as I was saying it's good to see so many healthy young saints sitting thicker on the ground than a bramble bush… Reminds me of the time Karmapa came to the dojo. You'd have thought it was Mick Jesus on the altar the place was so packed. And sitting too, without moving. A good thing to see, the visualization of mindfulness.

That's fine… and dandy too… when you have a seat to sit in. Sometimes, like right now for instance, why there isn't a single seat left. *Où je vais m'asseoir moi*? Where am I going to sit, for Pete's sake? I say it out loud. You never know, someone might hear me and give me his own place. After all what are saints for, if not for that?

I look down at Baobab on the floor below me and he looks up and says: Sit in the dressing room.

Sit in the toilet, adds someone else.

I look over at the guy. Never seen him before. I have been coming here near ten years now, and this guy who's just dropped through the skylight tells me to go sit in the toilet. My mind goes from amazement to indignation and rage in literally no time flat. I mean I have half a mind to kick him in the teeth, but being barefoot it might hurt the toes, so I turn away… and just then the kyosakuman nudges me with the stick and points it in the direction of the curtain. My rage, which came in no time flat, leaves at about the same speed and I smile and nod at the kyosaku-man and walk the other way. Today I am sitting in the dojo, no matter what. So I hustle myself a seat between Smartie the editor and Peppone the Buddha-statue thief, knees sticking into zafus, back against the altar, and wait for the bell.

Last time it was like this was when the Tibetans came for a visit. They all wore yellowish-orange robes and they sat facing outwards and this way they could see for themselves how beautifully we sat, backs straight, heads on shoulders and all that. It was a kind of jolly show-biz number and Yakumatsu himself gave us the kyosaku, and man did he ever lay it into us. Why, he hit us so hard our zafus flattened out like pancakes. Anyway, Karmapa was laughing so much he split his robe right up the crack of his ass, and it made a funny ripping sound… and then there was a kind of background mumbling – the Tibetans were estimating the damages – and then there was the ceremony and that was the best part, seeing the Karmapa's underpants and all.

The bell is rung and the master steps in and it's good to hear his voice again, all that silence was getting me down – it can get kind of boring especially silence you know – and now the master is saying The atmosphere here is very strong very deep… more logs you put on fire bigger the fire.

He keeps talking and the words flow by me like leaves in a breeze, the breeze blows this way and that and back again: …transmission of character… a person who impressed with character of Shakyamuni Buddha and no shadow between… seeing each other every day we do not separate life and death… The words drift off, then: Do not imitate… create the today of your own self… things of today are no-thought no-mind mushin hishiryo…

We enter the genmai hall sit down cross our legs again and chant the mealtime sutra and eat our soup… Once most of the people have got up and gone, I join Yaku at his table. There are two or three of us, Lamponéon and Virginie and some others and Yaku isn't looking too good, yellowish and tired, and no one is saying very much, just drinking coffee and smoking and after a bit I address him: How do you feel today Sensei?

Good not so good. Yaku pats his belly, Pancreas bad.

Sure, I muse, le mal du siècle, le pas mal du siècle… in the pancreas.

I must go to Japan, for an operation. An operation?

Yaku looks me in the eye and winks. I understand. Maybe yes maybe no. Is he alive or is he dead? like that koan has it.

Then I will come back.

I notice that Yaku doesn't wink this time. When are you going? I ask.

I go today.

Today? You already have the plane ticket?

He nods.

What airline are you taking?

I have private plane, he grins.

Oh come on.

True true. President Mitterand give me his plane. Then I come back. While Yaku goes through his mail, Virginie and I start talking about the teaching, about the Brussels sesshin and then about Yaku himself. He is in bad shape, Virginie says. He is in pain all the time – cancer of the pancreas. But he never complains. Except against the doctors. The doctors are always talking about operation, operation. But he doesn't want to hear about it…

Yaku gets to his feet and we enter the facing building, the secretary at his side, and stop at the elevator. Yaku steps through the big doors and he looks at me long and penetratingly and we do gassho, and I say, Have a good trip! and the door closes with a sudden clank, he on one side, me on the other, and that's that.

I am on the street and it's kind of windy, the clouds are being blown away and the sun is screwing in up there, sort of like in a Van Gogh, the sun is screwing the sky, the sky is screwing the atmosphere which is screwing the biosphere and right in the middle of this extraordinary screw-stuff we have – not the Lord Jehovah – but my own very self, screwing along with everyone else.

Back home, I find a letter from the States. Another editor. My friend and benefactor, old Chevalier, is still sending my stuff around. He doesn't give up… I open the letter with a certain amount of indifference… alas. It's from K… the publishers. A lady writing. Says I should practice more meditation. Make that breakthrough , Mister Dilly, she enjoins me. Perhaps were you to try meditating on a burning incense stick… I read the letter again, turn it upside down and read it once backwards and it still says the same thing. Ten years with AnuttaraSamyakSambodhi and she tells me I should try an incense stick… Patience, patience…

The phone. Hello? Long distance. Ah it's from the States. Albuquerque. Johnny Tree. My old friend and fellow bushman.

We exchange a few words about nothing much and that feeling of suspense I felt earlier comes back to me… Well, what's up Johnny? / I got some bad news for you. / Yeah? / It's to do with Peter. / Okay go ahead. / You know, Mike, he's been missing… for a long time. / Missing? How do you mean? / Missing in action, you know what I mean…

I take a deep breath, I know what he means.

How long's he been missing Johnny? / That's what I'm trying to tell you, it's been over six months now. / O Chriiiiiiist. Well, what happened? / We don't know. No one knows. Anyone could have done it.

I place the phone back in its cradle and rub my head and face with both hands. Then I take up my rakusu and slip it over my head... Feeling terrible... can't even breathe... my lungs have just been crushed. My brother is no more. Him too. And not even a body to go by this time.

22

Days go by and slowly turn into weeks. My relationship with Caroline has gone down the drain, and Chevalier my old sponsor is not providing anymore. Nothing happens that's worth writing home about. Right now it's early morning and I am seated in a blanket on the floor.

I drink down the coffee cold, too low to light the flame, pull on any pants any shirt and jacket, open the door and, neglecting to close it behind me, I enter the morning dish-water.

The bell rings and thoughts of Peter consume me, of Peter and me in the desert, with our guns and stuff… and I am not into zaso at all this morning.

I breathe in and out. If there's one thing I can do on this earth it's to breathe. It takes a long time, for everybody, but in the end it works out, you come back, and you hear, for the first time, the rain hitting the skylight pitter-patter, the ticktock of the clock, the barkbark of a dog…

Don't know how long we've been sitting here, breathing in and breathing out, like we're all at the oars heaving-ho, the shusso at the rudder, kyosakuman standing motionless in the wind, and I, myself, sitting in the back row… The guys up front are rowing okay today, you can feel them in the oars, in the planks, the mast, nuts, bolts and pulley blocks – you can feel everyone, everything…

Like the guy to my left… screwing up… nodding at the oar what. The First Mate whacks him on the head with the capstan bar and chucks him overboard, which is a good thing. This is no time to be messing around. My brother is out there and we must save him…

Don't know how long we've been at it, but now a north wind has started up and with the sails trimmed, there's no need to row anymore. Wow-y… I mean wu-wei…

Well that was great! A moment of respite in the storm. But of course moments of respite don't really help much… not in the long run in any case. I mean it doesn't save my brother. Like he once saved me…

Hands in my pockets, I head home through the slimy weather thinking of the time some years back when Peter and I were in the sagebrush the sun bright, the sky blue, without a cloud, without a problem, without a worry in the world – but not all the time. Like that time we were camped in the Poison Spider region, Wyoming USA, in a rundown shack built by the homesteaders some time before the cataclysm, made of planks and pasted over on the inside with moldy yellow-faded newspapers dating back to before the wars, the floor and shelves presently cluttered with our equipment, claimposts, posthole diggers, measuring chain, a Winchester… and Peter at the table going over a topographic map and beside him a roll of toilet paper and a handgun. I was sitting in the doorway, boots removed, wiggling my toes in the late afternoon sun and turning the pages of a magazine called *The Uranium Prospector*, to which we were subscribers, when an old Ford truck with out-of-state plates pulled up on the far side of the patio. About fifty yards due east, that is in the setting sun, and at that moment about eyelevel. It didn't look good. Anyone could tell that.

The man in the passenger seat climbed out lackadaisically and took a few steps in my direction. Peter meanwhile had crept over into the shadows and went ssshhh! and it was a scary moment, heart pounding hard, could hardly breathe, but I played it along… played down my brother's presence.

The man carried a gun at his side and wore a red bandana around his forehead, like an Indian. The other man stepped out from the driver's seat and he was wearing a hat and that's about all I could make out because the one in the foreground suddenly started shouting: Where's yer partner? / I'm alone! / Bullshit! shouted the man in the background. / What do you want? / We've come to re-POZZ-ESS our land! / Well, I shout back at the two-bit claimjumpers, it's not yours, it's ours! / Bullshit. / Who got here first? We did! Who has pedis possessio? We do! Squatters rights, damn right! All written up. / Up yer ass! / All written up in the register… the County Seat! In Rawlins! Damn right! So you can just buzz off –!

The man answered me with a bullet! Before I knew what was what he had pulled a gun and was shooting at me!

The bullet caught me in the leg, just below the knee, paralyzing me on the spot. Peter pulled me to cover by the armpits, and now we were both inside, Peter with the old Browning automatic he'd brought back from Korea, and me on the floor with the Winchester.

There was no time for thinking and so there was very little to remember. It was a little like when you're in zaso, nothing much to remember, except maybe some of the decor. Like the bullets flying all over the place… and like how Peter did the good shooting… Sure, he'd already done it in Korea many times, but what the hell he was good today unloading his clip so fast you couldn't count the shots had you tried. But then again I remember getting off a shot or two myself, not so fast, but it was a good rifle, better than their handguns at any rate.

Once the shooting stopped the head took over again, just like after zaso, and once more there was so much to think about, to worry about. There wasn't just my leg to look after, there were these two bodies out there, and one of them was still kicking, and we had to do something about that too.

And now I see myself, on the floor, a towel against my leg, my mouth mashing the same words, Hey Peter we just killed those guys, we just killed those guys…

Peter checked out my wound, with shaky hands himself, and said : We'll get you to the horse doctor over at Lee's, you'll be okay.

We killed those guys, I mumbled into the bloody towel.

Better you forget about it. Peter got up off his knees. Just think of them as missing in action, and you'll get over it.

So as I was saying, Peter was in okay shape and he took care of everything, like the good brother he was. He undressed the bodies, removed everything but their guns, and I sat and watched and didn't say anything. Maybe I

222

had lost my power of speech or maybe there was just nothing more to say…

Then I stood up on one foot and we had a little funeral and prayed to God, we were sorry by what we did and hoped we hadn't made any mistakes. Amen.

23

O fresh horrors from Hades.

JAMES JOYCE

It's that hour before awakening, a time filled with white and red horrors, dreaming, not so much about my brother as about my master, his shiny top, a kotsu pointing at my feet and I look up and see his face, mouth sunken like he's forgotten his false teeth or something… and now I am coming out of it and the moment is replaced with distant pretty sounds, a bird at the window, a flute in the meadow, a bell in the steeple and I open my eyes and immediately I feel this strange thing, like something is wrong when nothing is wrong, and the feeling, whatever it is, is not fluttering about in the brain, it's right inside, in my bones.

I head for the kitchen piss in the sink, run the water and do gassho. Then I head around the corner… and run right into Dagoba. The light is a dim grey and it's drizzling miserably and I look at Dagoba who is looking kind of like the white horror itself, shoulders bent under the drizzle and we are both heading in the same direction and we exchange a few words and then he tells me: Sensei is dead. He died in Tokyo sometime this morning.

Dead? Of course, I answer myself.

We walk in silence. Around the corner of bad times. The world grey, the houses crooked, shoulders like broken broomsticks.

The dojo is quiet. Everyone is seated, except Lamponéon who is at the altar installing a photo of Yaku beneath the plastic Buddha, and no one moves much, the garbage collector is quiet, so is the translator, and the editor, the secretary, the fellow whose mother is a bus-driver, and the other fellow, the one who got ripped off in Tangier, even Dalley himself for a change, sits quietly. Everyone is quiet, the clock has stopped ticking, the pigeons have stopped hopping. And then afterwards it's the same thing, just a little dust in the eyes, a little rot in the mouth, a little itch in the ear, a little wail in the mind…

24

Things of today are no-thought.

YAKUMATSU

The alarm rings twice and I rise up naturally before the third ring, and without thinking too much I turn on the heat, take up the razor, square myself in front of the mirror and shave.

The washed-out sky above, the wet pavement below, the closed café, the cold cemetery, the old trees sticking out over its walls, the sooty chimneys, the yellowish light of streetlamps, the black pharmacy window, the squatters' ruins…

And now we are in the dressing room and there are many of us this morning and yet we remove our clothes without much pushing and replace them with the white kimono from Japan, the black kolomo from China and the kesa from the Buddha in India, and with the oldest skin on top and the newest beneath, that is our underwear, we walk barefoot under the sky, over the pavement, under the little windbell in the doorway and into the dojo where we sit with our legs crossed, soles facing upwards, backbones straight, eyes noses tongues teeth fingers feet and toes all accounted for…

EPILOGUE

And so what was once Winter is now Spring and now it's Yaku's turn. He falls like ancient Rome, taking everything with him... But that's another story... Enough is enough... I need a drink... go to the Sélect... lean up against the bar... see this girl... bright eyes, a gentle face, smoking a Marlboro in a black cigarette holder... I order a beer, bum a cigar from my neighbor, and wait for the right moment...

Paris 1983

GLOSSARY

ANUTTARASAMYAKSAMBODHI: Ultimate awareness, hishiryo.

BASO: Ma-tsu, d. 788. Great Chan master and first to use the rough method on his disciples.

BODHISATTVA: A bodhisattva dedicates his life to helping others by participating in the social reality.

BUSSHO KAPILA: Mealtime sutra.

CHAN: Chinese for zen.

DAKINI: Female spirit who comes from the sky.

DHARMA: The universal law taught by Shakyamuni Buddha.

DOGEN: d. 1253. Great Japanese Soto master and author of the *Shobogenzo*.

DOJO: The place of practice: *Do*: the way; *jo*: the place.

DOKAN: Ring of the way. The continual repetition of the acts of one's life (see GYOJI).

EIGHTFOLD NOBLE PATH: Right vision – right thought – right speech – right action – right livelihood – right effort – right mindfulness – right samadhi.

GAITAN: Entrance area to the dojo.

GASSHO: A gesture of reverence and respect in which the palms of the hands are placed together in front of the lower part of the face.

GENMAI: Traditional rice soup eaten after the morning zazen. Consists of one portion of brown rice to one sixth leeks, celery branch, carrots, turnips and onions.

GENSHA: d. 908. Great Chan Soto master.

GYOJI: The continuous practice, with emphasis on *samu* or holy work without profit or goal. *Gyo* means to practice, *ji* means to continue, perpetuate and to protect.

HANNYA SHINGYO: *Heart Sutra*. This short sutra is chanted in all zen temples or dojos after zazen.

HARA: Lower abdomen.

HISHIRYO: Beyond thinking. Thinking from the bottom of non-thinking.
A monk came up to master Yakusan (d. 834) who was sitting in zaso and said: "Master, what do you think when you sit?" "I think not-thinking," Yakusan replied. "How do you think not-thinking?" "Hishiryo," Yakusan replied.
Hi means beyond, *shiryo* means thinking.

HOSAN: Official day off for the monks.

INKIN: Small, delicately shaped bell with handle. Struck with measured cadence by the inkin-ringer, when accompanying the master to and from the dojo, etc.

I SHIN DEN SHIN: From mind to mind. *I* means with; *shin* means mind; *den* means to transmit.

KALPA: Sanskrit word denoting eons of time.

KAN JI ZAI BO SATSU: First words chanted in the *Han-nya Shingyo*, "The Bodhisattva of true compassion…"

KANJI: Ideogram

KARMA: The totality of one's acts, plus the consequences. Karma is the law of cause and effect, and yet it is beyond causality, beyond destiny, for it can indeed be changed.

KARMAPA: d. 1982. Tibetan spiritual authority of the oldest Tulku lineage of Tibetan Buddhism and in the line of the transmission of the Vajrayana teachings.

KENDO: The way of the sword.

KESA: Monk's robe worn over left shoulder during zazen; made out of cotton, linen or silk; black, brown or grey in color, and symbol of the Buddha's robe.

KI: Energy, activity. *Ki* is located throughout the entire body, as well as in a mind capable of responding to a spiritual impulsion.

KINHIN: Walking zen done between two periods of sitting.

KOAN: Enigma or paradox. A tool often used to educate a disciple. In the Rinzai tradition it is used as a means for obtaining satori.

KOLOMO: Sometimes pronounced koromo. A black robe worn by monks and nuns. Similar to a black kimono, except for the size of the sleeves. A kolomo's sleeves are very large.

KOTSU: Curved-topped staff the master carries with him. Made of wood and varying in length between one and two feet.

KU: That emptiness from where everything comes.

KUSEN: The oral teaching given by the master during zaso.

KWATZ: A Rinzai war cry of pure energy which can be translated to mean "wake up!"

KYOSAKU: Stick for awakening. About one meter long and flattened at the end. The disciple is struck on the shoulder muscles on each side of the neck by the master or kyosakuman. A strong kyosaku, says Yakumatsu, can wake up body and mind.

LAMAISM: The Buddhism of Tibet.

MAHAYANA SUTRAS: The teaching of Shakyamuni Buddha originally recorded in Sanskrit, as opposed to Pali.

MAKYO: Devil visions in which one usually sees bodhisattvas and dakinis; some people can even hear them when they talk.

MONDO: Question and answer session between master and disciple.

MOKUGYO: Hollowed-out wooden drum carved in the

shape of a fish.

MUDRA: The pose of the hands during zaso. The hands rest, palms upwards, on the foot, against the belly, under the navel and in front of the hara. The thumbs touch, forming a spherical shape.

MUSHIN: No-mind.

MUSHOTOKU: Nothing to obtain, nothing to profit from.

NARAKA: Hell.

RAKUSU: A small kesa worn around the neck and over the chest.

RENSAKU: A series of blows given with the kyosaku on each shoulder.

RINZAI: Lin-chi, d. 867. Great Chan master and founder of the Rinzai school. His method of teaching was very fierce and direct.

SAMADHI: (*Zanmai* in Japanese). Complete concentration of mind and body.

SANPAI: A series of three prostrations. The feet, knees, hands (palms upwards), and forehead touch the ground.

SANGHA: An assembly of monks, nuns and lay practitioners who follow the way of Buddha and practice together.

SATORI: Awakening; a return to the normal condition, to one's true original nature.

SENSEI: A respectful, affectionate word for addressing the master; teacher.

SESSHIN: A period of intensive zaso practice.

SHIHO: Official document of transmission from master to disciple.

SHIKANTAZA: Concentrated sitting in the posture of zaso.

SHIKI SOKU ZE SHIKI: Form becomes form.

SHOBOGENZO: Title given to the monumental work by Dogen. It means "treasury-eye of the true teaching."

SHOKO: The burning of incense.

SHUSSO: The shusso is responsible for everything that happens in the dojo. Second in charge after the master.

SUTRA: Discourse of the Buddha. Writings that make up part of the Buddhist canon.

TOZAN: Tung-shan, d. 869. Great Chan master and founder of the Soto school.

TENZO: Head cook in a temple or monastery.

VIPASSANA: A Buddhist form of meditation practiced in the Theravada and based on developing "Right Mindfulness."

WU-WEI: A Taoist concept meaning nondoing as distinct from no-action (in the sense of immobility). In zen it means without thought of self, without purpose.

ZAFU: A round cushion filled with kapok and upon which one sits when in zaso.

ZAGU: A cloth the master or disciple spreads out on the floor before him so that he can make a prostration on it.

ZANMAI: See samadhi.

ZASO: Zazen.

ZAZEN: The practice of sitting facing a wall in a quiet place with legs crossed in the half or full lotus.

ZENDO: Another word for dojo.